Best Ever

Baking

Ann Nicol

© 2005 D&S Books Ltd
© 2010 Kerswell Farm Ltd

This edition published by Kerswell Books Ltd

Printed 2010

This book is distributed in the UK by
Parkham Books Ltd
Kerswell Farm,
Parkham Ash, Bideford
Devon, England
EX39 5PR

enquiries@parkhambooks.co.uk

ISBN: 978-1-906239-57-2

DS0120. Baking – Best Ever Recipes

Creative Director: Sarah King
Editor: Debbie Key
Project editor: Nicola Barber
Designer: Debbie Fisher
Photography: Colin Bowling/Paul Forrester

Printed in Singapore

Material from this book previously appeared in *100 Great Recipes - Baking*

1 3 5 7 9 10 8 6 4 2

Contents

introduction

Introduction

There's something extremely satisfying about real home baking and the sense of achievement you get when you have made a fresh batch of cakes for your family. The comforting aroma of baking that fills the house and the mouth-watering moment when you first bite into a golden crumbly cake, are well worth the effort.

We all lead busy lives these days and most people say they don't have time for home baking. The tradition of baking may end up becoming more of a hobby. But if you want to take time out from the stresses of modern life, why not indulge in the therapeutic delights of baking? There is no better way of relaxing than kneading a dough, or beating a fluffy, buttery mixture. If you are worried about giving your family manufactured foods containing chemical additives, colourings, preservatives and excess salt, you will find home baking solves this problem. You'll have total control over the ingredients you use in baking and, don't forget, there is a good range of organic and additive-free ingredients and free-range eggs now available in supermarkets.

100 Great Recipes Baking provides a delicious range of recipes for cakes, biscuits and teabreads, and you'll find sweet and savoury pastry dishes as well (ideal for packing into lunch boxes). You can be creative with yeasted breads and bakes, or make traditional favourites such as hot cross buns. Wholewheat flours need special treatment, so there is a separate section on these, including some vegetarian recipes, too. Traybakes are larger cakes baked in trays for cutting into squares. You will find this section useful if you are ever asked to bake for a charity stall or the school fête. For formal occasions, there are some mouth-watering gateaux requiring a little more preparation. Chocolate must be the most popular ingredient in baking, so I've included plenty of recipes using dark, white and milk chocolate, cocoa powder, grated, melted and chocolate chips. I have also added a recipe made from carob for those who are allergic to chocolate.

This book is aimed at those who are new to baking and also experienced bakers. In *100 Great Recipes Baking*, I have chosen step-by-step recipes with pictures, showing you how to create lovely bakes in easy stages. There are cakes for every occasion, some very quick and easy, some requiring a little more time. You'll find cakes for special occasions such as birthdays, or simple, plain cookies and teabreads that go well with a cup of tea. So, choose your favourite recipe and start baking now. Fill the kitchen with the aroma of freshly baked cakes and sit back and wait for the comments of admiration.

Tips for Success

Here are some baking tips that will help you to achieve the best results, so follow these for success.

Oven Temperatures

I usually begin each recipe with the oven temperature. It does make a difference if you preheat the oven to the correct temperature before placing the cake in to bake.

- Always preheat the oven in plenty of time, and arrange the shelves in the correct position in the oven.

- If you have a fan-assisted oven, these circulate hot air around the oven and heat up very quickly. For these ovens you will need to reduce the temperature by 10% and you may also need to reduce the cooking time as well. Follow your manufacturer's instruction leaflet and get to know the way your oven heats up for success.

- **TOO HOT** Remember, if the oven is too hot, the outside of a cake will burn before the inside has had time to cook.

- **TOO COOL** Remember, if the oven is too cool, this may cause cakes to sink or rise unevenly.

- Don't open the oven door until at least halfway through the baking time, or the rising process will be interrupted. This will cause a sudden drop in temperature which will stop the cake expanding and make it sink.

Tins

- Always use the size of tin stated in the recipe, or else your cakes will turn out too shallow, will peak, crack, or even sink in the middle.

- Choose good-quality, rigid, non-stick bake ware. If you are buying new tins, it is a good investment to pay a little more. Good-quality tins will last much longer and give better results. Cheaper bake ware, particularly baking sheets, may bend and buckle during baking.

Preparing Tins

Each recipe gives instructions on how to prepare and line the tins. These are important stages, so don't be tempted to skimp on these as the time and expense in making a cake may be wasted if you cannot turn the cake out of the tin.

- Tins without a non-stick finish need to be greased and lined before use.

- Non-stick tins need only a light greasing, but it is still advisable to line the bases of tins to ensure the cake can be released easily.

- Apply a thin film of melted vegetable margarine to tins using a pastry brush, or rub around the tin with kitchen paper and a little softened margarine.

- To line sandwich tins, place the tin on a sheet of non-stick or greaseproof paper and trace around the tin with a pencil. Cut around the shape and you will find this should fit the tin exactly.

- Deep, round tins for heavy fruit cake mixtures need to be double-lined around the base and sides. To do this, cut a piece of paper big enough to fold double and stand about 5cm/2 inches higher than the tin depth. Fold up the folded edge of the strip about 2.5cm/1 inch and snip with scissors along the folded piece in a slanting direction. Grease the tin and line the sides of the strip with the snipped edge at the base, lying flat. Place two rounds of paper on the base of the tin to cover the snipped edge.

- Non-stick paper does not require greasing and is a very useful paper as mixtures, even sugary ones, will not stick to it.

Checking Cooked Cakes

- The last part of a cake to cook is the centre, so after the baking time stated, check this area.

- For sponges, press the centre lightly with the fingertips. If the sponge is cooked, it should spring back easily and not leave an imprint; the sides of a sponge should also shrink away slightly from the sides of the tin.

- To test creamed or fruit cakes, insert a thin, warmed skewer into the deepest part of the cake. If the cake is cooked, it should come out perfectly clean with no mixture sticking to it. If there is mixture on the skewer, bake the cake for a little longer.

- Small cakes should be golden, risen and firm to the touch when pressed lightly in the centre.

Cooling the Cakes

- All freshly baked cakes are very fragile, so I have given times to allow them to stand in the tins to cool to firm them.

- After the cakes are firm, loosen the sides with a palette knife if necessary and turn them out to cool on a wire rack.

- Rich fruit cakes are very soft when newly cooked, so leave these in the tin for longer. Very rich fruit cakes, such as wedding cakes, should be left in the tins to cool completely to give a good shape to the edges.

- Peel away lining papers when the cakes are still warm, as they will then come away easily and keep the cake in good shape.

Storing Cakes

- Make sure cakes and cookies are completely cold before storing in an airtight tin, otherwise condensation will form in the tin and this can cause the cakes to go mouldy.

- Store cookies and biscuits in a separate tin from cakes. Cakes have more moisture and will make the biscuits go soft.

- Plastic food containers will encourage cakes to keep moist so are ideal for richer sponges, but an airtight cake tin is necessary to keep cookies and biscuits crisp and dry.

- Fatless sponges, such as Swiss rolls, will keep for only 1 or 2 days. Sponges with added fat will store for 3 days and richer cakes, such as creamed sponges, will keep for up to a week.

- Light fruit cakes will store for 2 weeks in a tin, but rich fruit cakes will keep for 1 month after cutting.

- Store undecorated rich fruit cakes in their baking papers, prick the surface and brush with a little brandy or rum before storing.

- To store a rich fruit cake, overwrap in clean greaseproof paper and seal with tape. Wrap in a double layer of foil and store in a cool dry place.

- Store cakes with fresh cream fillings and decoration in the refrigerator.

- If you don't have a large cake container, invert a large mixing bowl over the cake on a plate or work surface. As long as the bowl meets the flat surface, the cake will stay fresh.

Freezing Cakes

- Each recipe gives individual freezer notes, but most cakes freeze well undecorated.

- Completely cool each cake and overwrap in strong freezer film or foil to exclude as much air as possible.

- To thaw, completely unwrap cakes and thaw at room temperature on racks, allowing plenty of time for larger cakes.

Basic Baking Ingredients

- Both metric and imperial measures are given in the recipes in this book. It is very important to follow one set of measurements only. They are not exact equivalents, so don't mix the two measurements as the quantities in the recipe will be altered.

- Spoon measures are used throughout this book. Use the sets of plastic or metal measures sold specifically for this purpose and remember, all spoon measures should be level. Don't use kitchen tablespoons or teaspoons as the sizes of these differ and may be inaccurate.

Sugar

Sugar is added to cakes not just for sweetness, but also because it helps to produce a spongy texture and makes the cake tender. Always use the right type of sugar for the recipe:

- Caster sugar comes in white and golden unrefined varieties. It creams easily with fats and blends easily into light sponge mixtures.

- Demerara sugar is grainy and is often used for decorative toppings, or for recipes where sugar is dissolved over heat.

- Soft light and dark brown sugars cream well and are used in fruit cake recipes, or where richer colours and flavours are needed.

- Muscovado is the best soft, dark brown sugar. It is natural and unrefined, with an excellent dark colour and rich flavour for fruit cakes and gingerbreads.

- Granulated sugar comes in a coarse white or golden unrefined variety and is used for toppings as it does not dissolve easily in baking.

- Icing sugar is white and powdery, but it also comes in a lovely unrefined golden variety. Store icing sugar in a dry place, as it tends to absorb moisture. Always sift icing sugar before use, as it tends to forms lumps during storage.

Eggs

- Eggs should always be stored in the refrigerator, but you will get a better result if you allow them to stand at room temperature for 1-2 hours before using them for baking. Eggs at room temperature will whisk better and achieve more aeration.

- Don't use cold eggs straight from the fridge. If you are in a hurry, place them in a bowl and cover with warm water for 10 minutes to take away the chill.

- If you are separating egg whites for meringues, break them into a cup one at a time so that if there are any specs of yolk or pieces of shell in the cup, you can remove them easily.

- Sponges and meringues will whisk up to a greater bulk if you use eggs that are over 5 days old.

- Eggs sold as economy or value eggs can be used for baking, but they may be ungraded and of different sizes, such as very small, or a variety of large and small. For best results, stick to eggs graded as small, medium and large.

- Recipes containing raw eggs should not be eaten by babies, the very young, elderly people or pregnant women. Dried egg whites give excellent results and can be substituted in royal icing recipes.

Flour

Choosing the right flour for a recipe is vital.

- Plain flour provides the structure that makes the cake but contains nothing to make a cake rise. Richer cakes and pastries that do not need raising agents are made with plain flour.

- Self-raising flour has raising agents mixed into it that will make a cake rise. It is normally used for sponges and light mixtures that contain no fruit.

- Strong plain flour is used for breads and cakes baked with yeast. This flour makes a dough that will stretch further, to give a light, springy, open texture that contains air.

- Wholewheat and wholemeal flours contain all the bran from the wheat which gives a good texture with extra fibre and tends to keep cakes and breads moist. The nutty flavour of wholewheat flour makes marvellous fruit cakes, breads and pastries. You will need to add a little more liquid when using these flours, as the bran absorbs more fluids.

Raising Agents

These make cakes rise when added to flour and produce a light texture. It is important to be accurate when measuring them out.

- Baking powder is a ready-made mixture of bicarbonate of soda and cream of tartar. When liquid is added, the powder bubbles and produces carbon dioxide which expands with the heat of the oven and gives the cake an airy texture.

- Bicarbonate of soda is a gentler raising agent and is often used to give spicy mixtures a lift. It must be measured accurately, as adding too much will give a bitter flavour.

- Cream of tartar is a fast-acting raising agent that works the minute it touches liquid, so always bake the mixture as soon as possible after adding it.

- Self-raising flour contains baking powder. If you have only plain flour available, add $2\frac{1}{2}$ teaspoons of baking powder to 225g/8oz plain flour.

Fats

Fats give flavour and texture to cakes and improve their keeping qualities. Always use them at room temperature to make mixing easier.

- Butter and hard, block-type margarine can be interchanged in a recipe, but butter will always give a superior flavour, so don't stint for the sake of a few pennies.

- Soft-tub margarine is only suitable for all-in-one sponge recipes, where all the ingredients are added and mixed together in one bowl. Don't over-beat these recipes or use soft-tub margarine for recipes that require a lot of whisking or beating, as the mixture will become very wet and the cake will sink.

Dried Fruits

- Dried vine fruits are usually pre-washed and cleaned when bought, but you may find large pieces of stalk in some packs, so it is worth picking them over. For rich fruit cakes, such as Christmas cakes, dried fruit benefits from soaking in alcohol such as dark sherry, brandy or rum which will make the fruits plump and succulent. If you don't want to use alcohol, substitute orange juice instead.

- Glacé and crystallised fruits, such as cherries, ginger or angelica, need to be rinsed and dried before use to wash away their sugary coating. If you don't do this, the fruits may sink to the bottom of the cake during baking.

Spices

Dried spices bring cakes alive. Although they have a fairly long shelf life, remember they don't keep indefinitely.

- Spices gradually lose their aroma and flavour, so only buy in small quantities when you need them.

- Both light and heat affect the flavour of spices, so if you store them in clear glass jars, store these away from the light or keep them in a drawer.

- Store spices in a cool place, particularly if your kitchen is hot and steamy.

- Don't tip spices into mixtures straight from the jar as steam may get in and cause the spice to go damp and deteriorate.

Nuts

Nuts for baking can be an expensive purchase and as they deteriorate quickly, it is not advisable to buy them in large quantities. If you do have a large pack of nuts that you are not going to use immediately, store them in the freezer.

- Walnuts are very oily and will turn rancid quickly, so don't buy or store these in bulk. Just buy a small amount when you need them. Larger walnut halves are more expensive. If you need walnuts for chopping, buy cheaper walnut pieces which are usually sold at budget prices.

- Almonds can be bought whole, blanched, slivered, flaked or ground.

- Shelled almonds still have their skins on. If you need to remove these, place the nuts in boiling water for 2-3 minutes and you will find the nuts will slip out of the skins easily.

- Ground almonds have a fine powdery texture. If you run out of ground almonds, place whole or flaked almonds in a food processor and work until fine. Be careful not to over-blend them, as this will release the natural oils from the nuts.

Chocolate

Chocolate cakes are such a treat, so for a really professional finish and flavour, it is always advisable to buy the highest-quality chocolate you can find, although this will probably be the most expensive.

- The most expensive chocolate contains a higher percentage of real cocoa fat which gives a flavour and texture that far outweighs cheaper varieties. The amount of cocoa fat or solids contained in a bar will be marked on the wrapper of any good-quality chocolate.

- If chocolate gets too hot during melting, or comes into contact with water or steam, it will seize or stiffen and become an unmanageable ball, instead of a melted mixture. You can add a little vegetable oil or margarine, a teaspoon at a time, to the mixture to make it liquid again.

- To melt chocolate successfully, break the bar into small pieces and place them in a heatproof bowl over a bowl of warm, not hot, water. Make sure the bowl containing the chocolate is completely dry and that steam cannot get into it, as steam and water are the enemy of melted chocolate. Heat the water very gently and leave the bowl to stand for about 10 minutes. If the water gets too hot, the chocolate will reach a high temperature and loose its sheen.

- The microwave oven is an ideal tool for melting chocolate. Break into pieces and place in a microwave-proof bowl and melt gently on Low or Defrost settings in small bursts of 1-2 minutes, checking and stirring in-between.

- White chocolate is expensive and the most difficult to work with. It is best to grate it finely and keep the temperature very low when melting it.

- Cocoa powder needs to be cooked for the full flavour to be released, so blend it with boiling water to make a paste before adding to a recipe.

- Drinking chocolate is not the same as cocoa powder as it contains milk powder and sugar, so don't substitute this for cocoa powder as it will spoil the flavour of a cake.

Extra Recipes for Decorating Cakes

Royal Icing

Royal icing is used to pipe decorations on to cakes, or to cover Christmas or wedding cakes to form a snowy, white surface.

1 Put the egg whites in a large bowl and whisk with a fork lightly until bubbling. Sift in half the icing sugar with the lemon juice and beat well with a wooden spoon for about 10 minutes until smooth.

2 Gradually, sift in the remaining icing and beat again until thick, smooth and brilliant white.

3 Keep the royal icing covered with a damp cloth until you are ready to use it. For piping, place in a small greaseproof paper bag.

4 To cover a cake, spread over the top and sides of the cake with a palette knife, then smooth down over the sides, or flick into points with the palette knife to make a snowy effect. Leave the icing for 3 days to dry and become firm.

Almond Paste

Makes 450g/1lb

Ingredients:

100g/4oz icing sugar
100g/4oz caster sugar
225g/8oz ground almonds
1 egg
1 teaspoon lemon juice
1 tablespoon brandy

Almond paste is used to cover cakes that are going to be finished with royal or roll-out fondant icing. Almond paste protects and seals a cake and gives you the opportunity to fill in any cracks to make a perfectly flat surface before icing.

1 Stir the sugars and ground almonds together in a bowl. Whisk the egg, lemon juice and brandy together and mix into the dry ingredients.

2 Knead until the paste is smooth. Wrap in clingfilm and store in the refrigerator until needed.

Cook's tip:

The paste can be made 2-3 days ahead of time, but after that, it will start to dry out and become difficult to handle.

Tips for
Successful Cooking

- Use metric or imperial measurements only; do not mix the two.

- Use measuring spoons: 1 tsp = 5ml; 1tbsp = 15ml

- All spoon measurements are level unless otherwise stated.

- All eggs are medium unless otherwise stated.

- Recipes using raw or lightly cooked eggs should not be given to babies, pregnant woman, the very old or anyone suffering from or recovering from an illness.

- The cooking times are an approximate guide only. If you are using a fan oven reduce the cooking time according to the manufacturers instructions.

- Ovens should be preheated to the required temperature.

- Fruits and vegetables should be washed before use.

pastry

Treacle Tart

Family Favourite

I add grated apples to this traditional sticky tart, to help lower the sugar content. It is delicious served with lashings of dairy custard.

Pastry:

225g/8oz plain flour
50g/2oz butter or block margarine
50g/2oz white vegetable fat

Filling:

200g/7oz golden syrup
50g/2oz soft light brown sugar
100g/4oz white breadcrumbs
150/5oz dessert apple, peeled, cored and coarsely grated
Finely grated rind and juice of 1 small lemon

30 minutes preparation
25 minutes baking
Serves 6-8

1 Preheat the oven to 190°C/375°F/Gas 5 and place a baking sheet in the oven to heat. Grease a 23cm/9 inch pie plate or loose-based flan tin.

2 Sift the flour into a bowl and add the fat, cut into small cubes. Rub the fat into the flour with your fingertips, until the mixture resembles fine crumbs. Stir in 8 teaspoons of chilled water and mix to a soft dough. Wrap and chill for 15 minutes.

3 Cut away one-third of the pastry, then roll out the rest to line the dish. Trim away the edges and pinch into a decorative edge. Roll out trimmings with the reserved pastry to a long strip, about 25cm/10 inch long.

4 Cut into 8 thin strips and keep aside.

5 To make the filling, warm the syrup in a saucepan, then add all the remaining ingredients and stir well. Spoon into the pastry-lined dish and smooth level.

6 Twist the pastry strips and lay them across the filling in a lattice pattern. Press down the ends, then brush with milk. Place on the hot baking sheet and bake for 25-30 minutes until the pastry is crisp and the filling is golden.

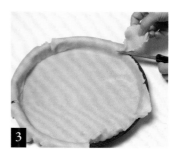

French Apple Tarts

Quick and Easy

If you need a super quick dessert, then rustle up these flaky, wafer-thin discs in under an hour. They are delicious served with scoops of vanilla ice cream.

Ingredients:

350g/12oz puff pastry
4 large dessert eating apples
Finely grated zest and juice of ½ lemon
4 tsp golden granulated sugar
25g/1oz butter
2 tbsp apricot jam, sieved, warmed

20 minutes preparation
20 minutes baking
Serves 4

1 Preheat the oven to 220°C/425°F/Gas 7. Grease a baking sheet then dampen slightly with water. Peel and core the apples.

2 Roll the pastry out thinly, then cut out four 15cm/ 6 inch circles using a saucer or small plate as a guide. Place the circles on the baking sheet. Slice the apples as thinly as possible and toss in the lemon juice and rind.

3 Arrange the apple slices (overlapping) on top of each pastry in a spiral pattern. Sprinkle a teaspoon of sugar evenly over the apples on each tart.

4 Cut the butter into small pieces and dot over the apples. Bake for 15-20 minutes or until the apples are tender and the pastry is golden. Transfer to four serving plates and brush the top of each tart with warmed apricot glaze.

Cook's tip:

- Sprinkling the baking sheet with water will create steam during the baking and will help the pastry to rise.
- If you don't have apricot jam for the glaze, use thin cut marmalade or clear honey instead.

Latticed Mince Pies

Easy Entertaining

Christmas would not be the same without mince pies and a glass of mulled wine. I make these well ahead of time, freeze them and bake them when needed, so they are always piping hot.

Pastry:

150g/5oz plain flour
150g/5oz self-raising flour
150g/5oz butter
25g/1oz vanilla caster sugar
1 medium egg, beaten
2 tbsp milk

Filling:

275g/10oz luxury fruit
mincemeat
1 tbsp dark rum or brandy
Icing sugar to serve

25 minutes preparation
15 minutes baking
Serves 12

1 Preheat the oven to 190°C/350°F/Gas 5. Grease a 12-hole bun tray.

2 Sift the flours into a bowl and add the butter cut into small cubes. Rub the fat into the flour until it forms fine crumbs. Stir in the sugar. Add enough egg and milk to bind into a soft dough. Knead until smooth, then wrap in clingfilm and chill in the freezer for 5 minutes.

3 Roll out the pastry to a thickness of 3mm/¹/₈ inch.

4 Cut out 12 circles using a 7.5cm/3 inch pastry cutter and press into the bun tins.

4 To make the filling, mix the rum or brandy into the mincemeat and fill each case three-quarters full. Gather up the trimmings and re-roll into thin strips.

5 Place the strips in a lattice pattern over the fruit filling, dampen the edges and press down. Bake for 15 minutes until the pastry is firm and golden. Dust with icing sugar to serve.

Cook's tip:

Freeze the uncooked pies directly in the bun tray, wrapped in foil. They keep for 3 months. To use, thaw thoroughly at room temperature, then bake as above.

Tarte au Citron

Freezer Friendly

I always serve this tart as a dinner party dessert. Light and refreshing, it is ideal after a heavy main course, plus you can make it ahead and chill it until needed, so it couldn't be easier to serve.

Pastry:

100g/4oz plain flour
50g/2oz butter
50g/2oz vanilla caster sugar
2 egg yolks

Filling:

2 lemons
4 eggs, beaten
175g/6oz caster sugar
150ml/¹/₂ pt double cream

35 minutes preparation
40 minutes baking
Serves 8

1 Grease a 23cm/9 inch flan tin. Put the flour and butter into a food processor or bowl and blend or rub in until the mixture resembles fine crumbs.

2 Add the sugar and egg yolks and mix to a soft dough. Pat the pastry into a circle large enough to line the tin.

3 Press into the tin, trim the edges and prick all over with a fork. Chill the tart in the freezer for 10 minutes. Preheat the oven to 190°C/375°F/Gas 5.

4 Line the pastry with greaseproof paper and weigh down with baking beans. Bake for 15 minutes until golden, then remove the beans and paper.

5 To make the filling, finely grate the rind and squeeze the juice from the lemons. Beat the eggs, sugar and cream together until smooth. Pour into the pastry case.

6 Reduce the oven temperature to 180°C/350°F/Gas 4. Bake for 40 minutes or until set. Leave to cool in the tin, then chill. Serve with whipped cream.

Cook's tip:

Cool and freeze, wrapped in foil. Keeps for 2 months.

Raspberry & Apple Turnovers

Family Favourite

These flaky pastries are equally delicious made with blackberries or blackcurrants instead of the raspberries, when they are in season.

Pastry:

250g/9oz puff pastry
1 egg, beaten
1 tbsp granulated sugar

Filling:

275g/10oz Bramley cooking apples, peeled, cored and chopped
50g/2oz caster sugar
15g/¹/₂oz butter
175g/6oz raspberries

30 minutes preparation
20 minutes baking
Serves 4

1 Preheat the oven to 200°C/400°F/Gas 6. Grease two baking sheets. To make the filling, put the apples, sugar and butter into a pan with 1 tablespoon of cold water. Bring to the boil then simmer for 5 minutes, stirring occasionally, until the apples are tender. Stir in the raspberries and spoon into a bowl to cool.

2 Roll out the pastry on a lightly floured surface to a 38x25cm/15x10 inch rectangle. Cut into six 12.5cm/5 inch squares with a sharp knife.

3 Divide the filling between the squares and dampen the edges of each square with water. Fold two opposite corners over to make a triangle. Pinch the edges to seal and press down with a fork to make a pattern.

4 Brush with a beaten egg and sprinkle the top with sugar. Place on the baking sheets and bake for 20-25 minutes until puffy and light golden.

Cook's tip:

Don't be tempted to overfill the pastries or the fruit filling may leak out.

Scotch Pies

Family Favourite

These tasty pies come from Scotland, where they are also called Mutton Pies. The pastry is made with oil which means it is easy to mould and super-crisp when baked.

Filling:

1 tbsp vegetable oil
1 small onion, finely chopped
225g/8oz lean minced lamb
½ lamb stock cube
A pinch of grated nutmeg
A few drops of
Worcestershire   sauce

Pastry:

175g/6oz plain flour
A pinch of salt
60ml/4 tbsp vegetable oil
2 tbsp milk, to glaze

45 minutes preparation
30 minutes baking
Makes 4 pies

1 To make the filling, heat the oil in a heavy-based pan. Add the onions and fry for 2 minutes to soften. Add the lamb and cook until browned for about 5 minutes. Crumble in the stock cube, 4 tablespoons of water and season with, salt, pepper, nutmeg and Worcestershire sauce. Cook over a low heat for 5 minutes until most of the water evaporates. Remove from the heat.

2 Preheat the oven to 200°C/400°F/Gas 6. Grease a 4-hole Yorkshire pudding tin. Sift the flour and salt into a bowl and add the oil along with 3 tablespoons of warm water. Mix to a soft dough and knead lightly.

3 Halve the dough and keep one half wrapped. Roll the other half out on a floured surface and cut out 4x15cm/ 6 inch rounds and use to line the tins. Roll out the remaining pastry and cut out four 9cm/3½ inch) rounds for the lids.

4 Divide the filling between the cases, brush the edges with milk and put the lids on top.

5 Seal and crimp the edges with thumb and forefinger. Make a hole in the centre of each lid and brush with milk. Bake for about 30 minutes or until golden. Serve warm or cold.

Classic Quiche

Freezer Friendly

A warm slice of quiche with a plate of salad makes the ideal quick lunch or supper dish. This one freezes well and is a good standby for unexpected visitors.

Pastry:

100g/4oz plain flour
A pinch of salt
25g/1oz white vegetable fat
25g/1oz block margarine

Filling:

2 tsp vegetable oil
1 small onion, finely chopped
100g/4oz smoked streaky bacon, trimmed, diced
75g/3oz Gruyère or strong Cheddar cheese, grated
2 eggs, beaten
125ml/4fl oz single cream
1 tsp French mustard

30 minutes preparation
35 minutes baking
Serves 4

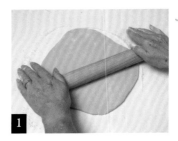

1 Preheat the oven to 180°C/350°F/Gas 4. Grease a 20cm/8 inch flan tin. Sift the flour and salt into a bowl and rub in the fat until it resembles fine crumbs. Add enough cold water to bind into a soft dough. Roll out the pastry thinly to a circle large enough to line the flan tin.

2 Lift the pastry into the tin and prick the base with a fork. Chill for 15 minutes. Fill with greaseproof paper and baking beans and bake blind for 15 minutes. Remove the paper and beans.

3 To make the filling, heat the oil and fry the bacon and onion until the bacon is crisp and the fat runs from it. Scatter into the pastry case with the cheese.

4 Whisk the eggs with the cream and mustard and season with salt and pepper. Pour into the pastry case over the filling and bake for 30-35 minutes or until golden and firm in the centre. Serve hot or cold with salad.

Cornish Pasties

Family Favourite

Cornish pasties are ideal for summer picnics. These ones have all the traditional ingredients, which keeps the filling moist and tasty.

Pastry:

500g/1lb 2oz shortcrust pastry
Beaten egg, to glaze

Filling:

175g/6oz lean braising steak, finely chopped
75g/3oz potato, peeled and coarsely grated
75g/3oz swede, peeled and coarsely grated
75g/3oz carrot, peeled and coarsely grated
75g/3oz onion, peeled and finely chopped
1 tbsp fresh parsley, chopped
A few drops of Worcestershire sauce

30 minutes preparation
40 minutes baking
Makes 6

3

1 Preheat the oven to 220°C/425°F/Gas 7. Lightly grease two baking sheets. To make the filling, mix all the ingredients together in a large bowl, then season with salt, pepper and a few drops of Worcestershire sauce.

2 Roll the pastry out on to a lightly floured surface to 3mm/1/8 inch thickness. Using a saucer as a guide, cut out six 15cm/6 inch rounds, re-rolling the pastry as necessary.

3 Brush the edges of each round with a little beaten egg. Divide the filling into six and spoon into the centre of each pastry round.

4 Carefully draw up the pastry edges to meet over the centre of the filling. Bring the pastry together and seal firmly.

5 Pinch the edges to make a fluted edge. Brush the pasties with beaten egg and place on the baking sheets. Bake for 10 minutes then reduce the temperature to 180°C/350°C/Gas 4 and bake for a further 30 minutes until golden. Serve hot or cold with green salad.

4

5

Apple Strudel

Easy Entertaining

These wafer-thin pastry layers are packed with a scrumptious apple filling and a hint of chocolate.

20 minutes preparation

30 minutes baking

Serves 6

Ingredients:

350g/12oz cooking apples, peeled, cored and thinly sliced
50g/2oz caster sugar
50g/2oz mixed dried fruit
150g/5oz (five sheets) filo pastry
50g/2oz butter, melted
25g/1oz white breadcrumbs
50g/2oz plain chocolate, grated
Icing sugar to dust

1 Preheat the oven to 200°C/400°F/Gas 6. Grease a large baking sheet. Mix the apples, sugar and fruit together and set aside.

2 Lay a sheet of filo pastry flat on a surface and brush with butter. Top with another pastry sheet and brush with butter. Make four layers of buttered pastry.

3 Sprinkle the breadcrumbs and chocolate down the centre of the pastry and sprinkle over the fruit mixture.

4 Roll the strudel up to enclose the filling. Place on the baking sheet, seam side down, and tuck in the ends. Brush the roll and the remaining filo sheet with butter, cut into strips and arrange on top of the roll in loose folds.

5 Bake for 30 minutes until the pastry is crisp and golden. Serve sifted with icing sugar.

Cook's tip:

- If you don't have a large baking sheet, bend the strudel round into a horseshoe shape to fit the tray.
- Keep the unused pastry covered with clingfilm or a damp cloth until needed.

Flaky Tuna Slice

Family Favourite

This is another useful recipe for packing into lunch boxes. Alternatively, serve the slice piping hot with lots of green salad.

Pastry:

**350g/12oz pack frozen puff
   pastry, thawed if frozen
1 egg, beaten**

Filling:

**1 tsp vegetable oil
100g/4oz button mushrooms,
   sliced
1 small leek, sliced
1 stick celery, sliced
225g/8oz can tuna, drained
25g/1oz white breadcrumbs
100g/4oz mozzarella cheese,
   cubed**

20 minutes preparation
30 minutes baking
Serves 6

1 Preheat the oven to 220°C/425°F/Gas 7. Roll out the pastry to a 30cm/ 12 inch square, then cut the pastry square in half.

2 Lightly flour one pastry half and using a sharp knife, cut a series of slits along the centre to within 1cm/1/2 inch of the cut edge.

3 To make the filling, heat the oil in a pan and lightly fry the vegetables for 5 minutes until softened. Cool in a bowl, then add the drained tuna,

breadcrumbs and cheese. Dampen a baking sheet and place the plain pastry strip on the sheet.

4 Spread the filling to within 2.5cm/1 inch of the border. Place the slashed strip of pastry carefully over the filling to cover and match the edges. Dampen and seal the edges then flute.

5 Brush the pastry with beaten egg and bake above the centre of the oven for about 30 minutes.

yeast
bakes

Herby Dough Balls

Easy Entertaining

These light little rolls are so versatile. I serve them with hearty winter soups or bake a few trayfulls to serve with barbecues.

Ingredients:

400g/14oz strong white bread flour
1 tsp salt
2 tbsp mixed dried herbs
1x7g sachet easy-blend yeast
50ml/2fl oz olive oil
200ml/7fl oz lukewarm water
1 tbsp melted butter

20 minutes preparation, 1 hour rising
20 minutes baking
Makes 16 rolls

1 Place the flour, salt and herbs in a large bowl and stir in the dried yeast powder. Make a well in the middle and add the olive oil and water.

2 Mix to a soft dough. Knead for 10 minutes by hand or 5 minutes in a mixer with a bread hook. Knead until soft and smooth on a floured surface.

3 Divide in half, then divide each half into 8 pieces. Grease two 20cm/8 inch loose based sandwich tins.

4 Roll each piece into a smooth ball and place in the tins. Leave enough space for the dough to expand. Cover with oiled cling wrap and leave for 1 hour or until doubled in size.

5 Preheat the oven to 200°C/400°F/Gas 6. Brush the tops with melted butter and bake for 20 minutes until golden and springy.

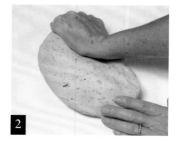

Cook's tip:

Add 1 clove of crushed garlic and 1 tablespoon of freshly chopped herbs to 50g/2oz melted butter and drizzle over the bread. Serve warm.

Cottage Loaf

Family Favourite

There's nothing to beat warm, crusty home-made bread, straight from the oven. This old-fashioned loaf is great for serving with soups, or simply enjoy it sliced and buttered.

Ingredients:

25g/1oz white vegetable fat
500g/1lb 2oz strong white flour
2 tsp salt
2 tsp caster sugar
1x7g sachet easy-blend yeast
1 tbsp salt

15 minutes preparation
1 hour 30 minutes rising
30 minutes baking
Makes 1 loaf

1 Cut the fat into small cubes. Stir the flour, salt and sugar together in a bowl and rub the fat into the flour until it forms fine crumbs. Stir in the yeast powder and add 300ml/1/2pt lukewarm water. Mix to a soft dough, then turn out on to a floured surface and knead for about 10 minutes until smooth and elastic.

2 Return to the bowl and cover with clingfilm. Leave in a warm place for 1 hour or until doubled in size. Knead the dough to knock out all the air.

3 Preheat the oven to 220°C/425°F/Gas 7 and grease a baking sheet. Shape

the dough into two balls, one using two-thirds of the dough, and a smaller one using one-third of the dough.

4 Place the large ball on the baking sheet, then place the smaller one on top. Flour a wooden spoon handle and use it to make a hole through the centre of both balls.

5 Cover and leave to double in size for about 30 minutes. Dissolve the salt in 2 tablespoons of water and brush all over the bread. Sprinkle lightly with flour and bake for 30-35 minutes until the bread sounds hollow when tapped. Cool on a wire rack.

Pizza Base

Easy Entertaining

Everyone loves a pizza! This plain white base is thin and crispy and you can try adding your own toppings and variations too, all at a fraction of the cost of a bought one.

Base:

225g/8oz strong white bread flour
1/2 tsp salt
25g/1oz vegetable margarine
2 tsp easy-blend yeast

Topping:

6 tbsp tomato pizza sauce
1 large beefsteak tomato, sliced
1 red pepper, sliced
50g/2oz salami, sliced
50g/2oz button mushrooms, sliced
100g/4oz artichoke hearts, sliced
50g/2oz canned anchovies, drained, sliced
25g/1oz black olives, sliced
50g/2oz mozzarella cheese, grated

30 minutes preparation, 1 hour rising
25 minutes baking
Serves 4

1 Sift the flour and salt into a large bowl and rub in the margarine until the mixture resembles fine crumbs. Stir in the easy-blend yeast and 150ml/1/4 pt lukewarm water and mix to a soft dough.

2 Knead the dough for 5 minutes until soft and smooth. Return to the bowl, cover with clingfilm and leave for about 1 hour until doubled in size.

3 Preheat the oven to 220°C/425°F/Gas 7. Grease a large baking sheet. Turn the dough out on to a floured surface and punch it to knock out the air. Knead until smooth, then roll out to a 30cm/12 inch round and place on the baking sheet.

4 Spread the dough with tomato sauce and top with sliced tomatoes. Arrange the topping ingredients, then scatter with grated cheese.

5 Bake for 20-25 minutes until the base is crisp and the topping is golden and bubbling. Cut into wedges and serve immediately.

Sun-dried Tomato Bread

vegetarian

Tomato bread is delicious served with cheeses and cold meats, or cut into strips and served with bowls of olives to accompany drinks.

Ingredients:

575g/1lb 4oz strong white bread flour
10ml/2 tsp salt
1x7g sachet easy-blend yeast
5 tbsp olive oil
300ml/¹/₂pt lukewarm water
1 tbsp coarse sea salt
225g/8oz sun-dried tomatoes, coarsely chopped

30 minutes preparation
1 hour rising
20 minutes baking
Makes 2 flat loaves

1 Put the flour in a bowl and stir in the salt and the dried yeast powder. Add four tablespoons of olive oil with the lukewarm water and stir to make a soft dough.

2 Knead the dough by hand for 10 minutes, or in a mixer with a dough hook for 5 minutes until smooth and elastic. Cover in clingfilm and leave for about 1 hour until doubled in size.

3 Turn the dough out on to a floured surface and punch it back to knock out all the air. Knead in the chopped tomatoes until evenly combined, then cut the dough in half.

4 Roll each piece out to an oblong measuring 20cm/ 8 inchx15cm/6 inch. Grease two baking sheets and place one dough piece on each. Brush with the remaining tablespoon of olive oil and make shallow diamond-shaped slashes across the top with a sharp knife.

5 Preheat the oven to 220°C/425°F/Gas 7. Cover the dough with oiled clingfilm and leave until doubled in size. Remove the wrap and sprinkle with sea salt. Bake for 20 minutes until the bread sounds hollow when tapped and it is browned.

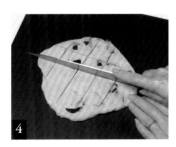

Grant Wholewheat Loaf

No Fat

This wholewheat bread was originated by Doris Grant, who was a health-food campaigner in the 1940s. This loaf is very easy to make as it needs only one rising.

Ingredients:

700g/1½lb strong wholewheat bread flour
5ml/1 tsp salt
1x7g sachet easy-blend yeast
2 tsp molasses or dark treacle
2 tsp salt, to glaze

15 minutes preparation, 1 hour rising
25 minutes baking
Makes 1 loaf

1 Grease a 900g/2lb loaf tin. Mix together the flour and salt into a bowl. Sprinkle in the yeast powder and continue to mix.

2 Make a well in the centre of the flour and pour in the treacle and 425ml/14fl oz of lukewarm water. Mix with a dough hook, or by hand, to make a soft, slightly wet dough. Knead until the dough leaves the sides of the bowl clean and feels elastic.

3 Place the dough in the tin and cover with oiled clingfilm and leave to double in size for about 1 hour. Preheat the oven to 200°C/400°F/Gas 6.

4 Blend the salt with 2 tablespoons of water and brush over the top of the loaf. Bake for about 35 minutes. Test to see if the bread is cooked by tapping with the knuckles. The bread should sound hollow.

Cook's tip:

Add your own topping: sprinkle the loaf with 1 tablespoon of cracked wheat, oatmeal or poppy seeds.

Bread Dough Sausage Rolls

Party Special

This is a very economical way of making sausage rolls for a crowd. If you roll the dough thinly, you can make even more cocktail-sized sausage rolls.

Ingredients:

25g/1oz white vegetable fat, diced
500g/1lb 2oz strong white flour
2 tsp salt
2 tsp caster sugar
1x7g sachet easy-blend yeast

450g/1lb pork sausagemeat
1 tbsptomato ketchup
1 tbsp mustard
A few drops Worcestershire sauce
50g/2oz red Leicester cheese
1 egg, beaten

1 hour preparation
25 minutes baking
Makes 32

1 Stir the flour, salt and sugar together in a bowl and rub the fat into the flour until it forms fine crumbs. Stir in the yeast powder and add 300ml/1/2pt lukewarm water. Mix to a soft dough and turn out on to a floured surface. Knead for 10 minutes until smooth.

2 Return to the bowl and cover with clingfilm. Leave in a warm place for 1 hour or until doubled in size. Knead the dough to knock out all the air.

3 Preheat the oven to 220°C/425°F/Gas 7 and grease two baking sheets. Roll the dough into a rectangle 50x23cm/20x9 inches. Cut the dough in half lengthways. Mix the mustard, ketchup and sauce together and spread over the dough. Shape the sausagemeat into two 50cm/ 20 inch lengths.

4 Place one piece of sausagemeat on each strip of dough then sprinkle with the cheese. Roll the dough up around the filling and smooth each piece out, rolling gently with your palms.

5 Cut each roll into 16 pieces, slash with a knife then brush with beaten egg. Place the rolls on the baking sheets and leave to rise for 30 minutes. Bake for 25 minutes until golden and puffy.

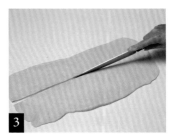

Chelsea Buns

Easy Entertaining

Ingredients:

250g/9oz strong plain flour
¹/₂ tsp salt
1x7g sachet easy-blend yeast
25g/1oz caster sugar
100ml/4fl oz milk
1 egg, beaten
15g/¹/₂oz butter, melted

Filling:

15g/¹/₂oz butter, melted
25g/1oz soft light brown sugar
¹/₂ tsp mixed spice
100g/4oz mixed dried fruit
2 tbsp golden syrup

15 minutes preparation
35 minutes rising
20 minutes baking
Makes 9

1 Grease an 18cm/7 inch square tin. Stir the flour, salt, yeast and sugar together. Stir the melted butter into the milk, beat in the egg, then pour into the flour and mix to a soft dough.

2 Turn the dough out on to a floured surface and knead until smooth for about 5 minutes. Roll out into a square 30x23cm/12x9 inch and brush with melted butter.

3 Scatter over the sugar, spice and dried fruit. Roll up like a Swiss roll from the longest side.

4 Cut the roll into 9 equal slices and place, cut side down, in the tin. Cover and leave to rise for 35 minutes until doubled in size.

5 Preheat the oven to 190°C/375°F/Gas 5. Bake for about 20 minutes or until light golden. Brush with syrup while the buns are still warm, then cool in the tin for 5 minutes. Turn out to cool on a wire rack, then pull apart.

Cook's tip:

If you don't have syrup available for a sticky glaze, dissolve together 2 tablespoons each of milk, water and sugar. Simmer for 2 minutes and brush over the hot buns.

Hot Cross Buns

Family Favourite

Home-made hot cross buns are really special. If you are short on time, make the dough ahead and freeze it in the tray, ready to bake for breakfast on Easter Day.

Pastry:

450g/1lb strong white bread flour
50g/2oz wholewheat flour
1 tsp salt
1 tsp ground cinnamon
1 tsp ground nutmeg
1 tsp ground mixed spice
50g/2oz soft light
 muscovado sugar
1x7g sachet easy-blend yeast
50g/2oz butter, melted
250ml/9fl oz milk
1 egg, beaten
175g/6oz mixed dried fruit

Crosses:

75g/3oz shortcrust
 pastry

Glaze:

1 egg, beaten
50g/2oz caster sugar

40 minutes preparation
1 hour 30 minutes rising
25 minutes baking
Makes 12

1 Sift the flours, salt and spices into a bowl. Stir in the sugar and yeast. Whisk the melted butter with the milk and the egg. Add to the bowl and mix to a soft dough. Knead for 5 minutes until smooth.

2 Knead in the fruit, then put the dough in a bowl and cover with lightly oiled clingfilm. Leave in a warm place for about 1 hour until doubled in size.

3 Grease a large baking tray or meat roasting tin. Cut the dough into 12 pieces and roll each one into a smooth ball. Space well apart in the tin.

Cover and leave to double in size for about 30 minutes.

4 Preheat the oven to 200°C/400°F/Gas 6. Brush the buns with a beaten egg. Roll the pastry thinly and place a line along the buns, then repeat the other way to make crosses. Bake for 20-25 minutes until risen and golden.

5 Heat the sugar in 2 tablespoons of water until dissolved. Turn the buns out of the tray while still hot and brush the warm buns with the glaze.

Cinnamon Ring

Easy Entertaining

A slice of this sticky cake brightens up any lunch box.

Ingredients:

350g/12 oz strong plain flour
1/2 tsp salt
1x7g sachet easy-blend yeast
25g/1oz caster sugar
15g/1/2oz butter, melted
100ml/4floz milk
1 egg, beaten

Filling:

100g/4oz no-soak dried
  apricots, chopped
75g/3oz butter, softened
50g/2oz soft light brown
  sugar
1 tsp ground cinnamon
50g/2oz raisins
50g/2oz glacé cherries
50g/2oz flaked almonds
2 tbsp clear honey

30 minutes preparation
1 hour rising
25 minutes baking
Serves 8

1 Stir the flour, salt, yeast and sugar together in a bowl. Stir the melted butter into the milk, beat in the egg, then pour into the flour and mix to a soft dough.

2 Turn the dough out on to a floured surface and knead until smooth for about 5 minutes. Return to the bowl and cover with oiled clingfilm. Leave until doubled in size.

3 Punch the air out of the dough and then roll out to a rectangle 30x22cm/12x8 1/2 inches. Spread with the softened butter then mix the

sugar and cinnamon with the dried fruits and scatter over the surface.

4 Roll up from the long side, like a Swiss roll.

5 Cut in half lengthways and then twist the two halves together. Form into a ring. Place on a greased baking sheet and cover with clingfilm for about 1 hour or until doubled in size.

6 Preheat the oven to 200°C/400°F/Gas 6. Bake for 25 minutes until golden. Brush with honey while still warm.

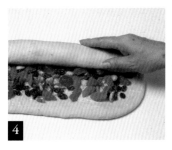

Cheesy Breadsticks

Easy Entertaining

Make your own crisp breadsticks to serve before an Italian meal. They are delicious served with dips and olives.

Ingredients:

350g/12oz strong white bread flour
100g/4oz strong wholewheat flour
25g/1oz finely grated Parmesan or strong Cheddar cheese
2 tsp salt
1x7g sachet easy-blend yeast
75ml/2½ fl oz olive oil
225ml/8fl oz lukewarm water

To Finish:

1 egg, beaten
1 tbsp poppy seeds
1 tbsp sesame seeds
25g/1oz finely grated Parmesan or strong Cheddar cheese

30 minutes preparation
1 hour rising
25 minutes baking
Makes 32 breadsticks

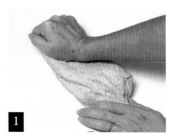

1 Place all the dough ingredients in a bowl and mix with a bread hook for 5 minutes to a soft dough. Alternately, mix by hand and knead for 10 minutes until soft and smooth.

2 Preheat the oven to 200°C/400°F/Gas 6. Grease two baking sheets. Divide the dough into 32 strips 1 cm/½ inch wide and about 25cm/10 inches long.

3 Roll the strips between the palms of your hands to make smooth, neat oblongs.

Beat the egg with a tablespoon of water and brush over each breadstick.

4 Place the sticks on the baking sheets and sprinkle one-third with grated cheese, one-third with poppy seeds and one-third with sesame seeds. Cover with oiled clingfilm and leave until doubled in size for about 30 minutes.

5 Bake for about 15 minutes until crisp. Keep in a tin or wrapped in foil until needed.

fruit and nut cakes

Irish Cake

Family Favourite

This dark, sticky fruit cake keeps moist for up to two weeks, so it's handy to have in the cake tin to share with friends. Serve it sliced and buttered with a good, strong cup of tea

Ingredients:

50g/2oz glacé cherries, halved
320g/12oz mixed dried fruit
Finely grated rind of 1 lemon
9 tbsp Guinness or stout
100g/4oz butter, softened
100g/4oz dark soft brown sugar
2 eggs, beaten
1 tbsp dark treacle
225g/8oz self-raising flour
1 tsp ground mixed spice
1 tbsp clear honey
1 tbsp demerara sugar

10 minutes preparation
50 minutes baking
Serves 12

1 Place the cherries, fruit and lemon rind in a saucepan with 8 tablespoons of stout. Heat to just below boiling. Simmer for 3 minutes, then pour into a bowl and cool for 30 minutes.

2 Preheat the oven to 180°C/350°F/Gas 4. Grease and line the base of a 20cm/8 inch round cake tin. Place the butter and sugar in a bowl and beat until light and fluffy.

3 Whisk in the eggs, adding a little flour with each. Add the treacle, flour, spice, fruit and 1 tablespoon of stout. Stir

together until the mixture is smooth.

4 Spoon into the tin, level the top, then make a dip in the centre. Bake for about 50 minutes, until a skewer inserted into the centre comes out cleanly. Leave in the tin for 10 minutes then cool on a wire rack. Wrap in foil or store in a cake tin for 2 days before eating. Brush the top with honey and sprinkle with sugar.

Rubbed-in Light Fruit Cake

Family Favourite

This is a really easy cake for beginners to make. There is nothing complicated about it, and it always turns out light and even.

Ingredients:

1 large carrot
225g/8oz self-raising flour
1/2 tsp mixed spice
150g/5oz butter or block margarine
175g/7oz mixed dried fruit

100g/4oz soft light brown sugar
2 eggs, beaten
3 tbsp milk
1 tbsp demerara sugar

25 minutes preparation
55 minutes baking
Serves 8

1 Preheat the oven to 180°C/350°F/Gas 4. Grease a deep 18cm/7 inch round tin and line the base with non-stick baking paper.

2 Peel the carrot and grate it finely. Sift the flour and spice into a mixing bowl, add the butter or margarine and cut it into small cubes.

3 Rub the fat into the flour with your fingertips until the mixture resembles fine breadcrumbs. Stir in the sugar dried fruit, and grated carrot. Make a hollow in the centre

and add the beaten egg and milk. Beat with a wooden spoon until it forms a soft dropping consistency.

4 Spoon into the tin and smooth level. Make a dip in the centre and bake for 45-55 minutes or until a warmed skewer inserted into the centre comes out cleanly.

5 Leave in the tin for 5 minutes, then turn out to cool on a wire rack. Peel away the lining paper, then sprinkle with sugar and serve sliced.

Cook's tip:

You'll need to use butter or block margarine in this cake. Soft-tub margarine will make the mixture too wet and the fruit may sink.

Buttery Danish Almond Cake

Freezer Friendly

This buttery cake combines two interesting textures: a plain, light and delicate sponge with a delicious, crunchy almond topping.

15 minutes preparation

40 minutes baking

Serves 8

Ingredients:

150g/5oz butter or block margarine
150g/5oz golden caster sugar
1 tsp almond essence
25g/1oz ground almonds
1 tsp lemon juice
2 eggs
150g/5oz self-raising flour
1 tbsp milk
25g/1oz flaked almonds
1 tbsp icing sugar

1 Preheat the oven to 180°C/350°F/Gas 4. Grease an 18cm/7 inch round cake tin and line the base with non-stick baking paper.

2 Beat the butter with the caster sugar and the essence until light and fluffy, then beat in the ground almonds and lemon juice.

3 Beat in the eggs, a little at a time, then fold in the flour with the milk and mix until smooth. Spoon into the tin, smooth the top level.

4 Scatter with the flaked almonds. Sift the icing sugar over the almonds and bake for 35-40 minutes until firm to the touch. Leave in the tin for 5 minutes then cool on a wire rack.

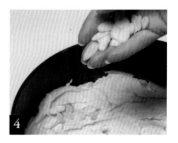

Cook's tip:

Add the beaten eggs in small batches, a little at a time. This will stop the mixture from separating or curdling, which will make the cake heavy.

Banana & Walnut Teabread

Family Favourite

Banana teabread is always popular and is a great way to use up ripe bananas.

Ingredients:

225g/8oz self-raising flour
1/4 tsp bicarbonate of soda
A pinch of salt
375g/14oz ripe bananas in their skins
300g/4oz walnut pieces
75g/3oz butter or block margarine
175g/6oz golden caster sugar
2 eggs, beaten

10 minutes preparation
1 hour 15 minutes baking
Serves 8

1 Preheat the oven to 180°C/350°F/Gas 4. Grease and line the base of a 900g/2lb loaf tin.

2 Sift the flour, bicarbonate of soda and salt together. Peel the bananas and mash them with a fork until softened. Chop the walnuts coarsely on a board.

3 Beat the butter and sugar together until light and fluffy. Beat the eggs into the mixture a little at a time, adding a teaspoon of flour with each batch.

4 Fold in the mashed bananas, flour and nuts and mix until smooth. Spoon into the tin and bake for 1 hour 15 minutes, or until a skewer inserted into the centre comes out cleanly with no mixture sticking to it.

5 Cool in the tin for 10 minutes then turn out and peel away the lining papers. Store in an airtight tin, or wrap tightly in foil.

Cook's tip:

Don't buy walnut halves for this recipe, as these are expensive. Packets of mis-shaped walnut pieces are much cheaper.

Dundee Cake

Easy Entertaining

This long-keeping cake is ideal to make ahead for a special family tea, or as a guess-the-weight cake for a raffle. I think it also makes a great New Year's present.

30 minutes preparation
2 hours baking
Serves 8

Ingredients:

400g/14oz mixed dried fruit
50g/2oz ground almonds
150g/5oz butter
150g/5oz golden caster
    sugar

Finely grated zest of 1 lemon
3 eggs, beaten
100g/4oz plain flour
50g/2oz whole almonds,
    skinned

1 Preheat the oven to 180°C/350°F/Gas 4. Grease and line the base and sides of an 18cm/7 inch round, deep cake tin.

2 Place the dried fruits in a bowl with the ground almonds and toss the fruit to coat it evenly.

3 Beat the butter and sugar and lemon zest together until light and fluffy. Whisk in the eggs, a little at a time, adding a teaspoon of flour with each addition.

4 Sift the remaining flour into the bowl and add the dried fruit. Fold together with 1 tablespoon of cold water until smooth and even.

5 Spoon the mixture into the tin, make a slight hollow in the centre, then smooth level. Arrange the almonds over the surface in circles.

6 Bake for 1 hour, then reduce the heat to 150°/300°F/Gas 2 and bake for a further hour, or until a skewer inserted into the centre comes out cleanly. Cool in the tin for 10 minutes then turn out to cool on a wire rack.

Cook's tip:
Store in an airtight tin for a week to improve the flavour.

Sultana Gingerbread Loaf

spicy

These dark, sticky, ginger slices couldn't be easier to make. Just melt the mixture together in a saucepan.

Ingredients:

100g/4oz butter or block margarine
100g/4oz light muscovado sugar
50g/2oz black treacle
50g/2oz golden syrup
150ml/¼pt milk
200g/7oz plain flour
1 tsp ground cinnamon

1 tbsp ground ginger
1 tsp bicarbonate of soda
2 eggs, beaten
75g/3oz sultanas

Frosting:

½ lemon
100g/4oz icing sugar
50g/2oz unsalted butter, softened

25 minutes preparation
40 minutes baking
Serves 8

1 Preheat the oven to 180°C/ 350°F/Gas 4. Grease and line the base of a 900g/2lb loaf tin with non-stick baking paper.

2 Put the butter, sugar, treacle and syrup in a saucepan and heat gently until all the ingredients are melted and blended. Cool slightly, then whisk the milk into the warm ingredients.

3 Sift the flour, spices and bicarbonate of soda into a bowl and make a well in the centre. Pour in the syrup mixture, then add the beaten eggs and whisk until smooth.

4 Add the sultanas and pour the mixture into the prepared tin. The mixture will have the consistency of a batter. Bake for 40 minutes or until a skewer inserted into the centre comes out cleanly.

5 Cool in the tin for 10 minutes, then turn out to cool on a wire rack.

6 To make the frosting, finely grate the zest from the lemon and squeeze 1 tablespoon of juice. Beat the butter with the icing sugar until light and fluffy, then add the lemon zest and juice. Spread over the top of the cake.

Walnut Layer Cake

Easy Entertaining

This moist, nutty cake, layered with vanilla buttercream, is perfect for a special occasion. It's ideal if you are asked to help make teas for the cricket team.

Ingredients:

225g/8oz self-raising flour
1 tsp baking powder
225g/8oz soft-tub margarine
225g/8oz soft light brown sugar
75g/3oz walnuts, finely chopped
4 eggs
1 tbsp black treacle

Decoration:

75g/3oz unsalted butter
1 tsp vanilla essence
175g/6oz icing sugar
175g/6oz fondant icing sugar
Walnut halves to decorate

30 minutes preparation
25 minutes baking
Serves 12

1 Preheat the oven to 160°C/325°F/Gas 3. Grease and line the bases of two 20cm/8 inch deep sandwich tins with non-stick baking paper. Sift the flour and baking powder into a bowl and add all the remaining cake ingredients.

2 Beat together for 2 minutes until smooth, then divide into the tins and spread level. Bake for 25-30 minutes until golden and springy to the touch. Turn out of the tins and cool on a wire rack. Cut each cake in half horizontally.

3 For the decoration, beat the butter, essence and icing sugar together until smooth. Spread thinly over one sponge half and sandwich a layer on top. Continue layering the sponges with the buttercream.

4 Place the cakes on a serving plate. Mix the fondant icing sugar with 1-2 teaspoons of water to make a thin consistency. Spread over the top of the cake, allowing the icing to drizzle down the sides. Place walnut halves in a circle on top of the cake.

Cook's tip:

Freeze the layers sandwiched with buttercream, but undecorated. Keeps for 2 months.

Apricot & Marmalade Loaf

Freezer Friendly

20 minutes preparation
40 minutes baking
Serves 8

Ingredients:

25g/1oz orange marmalade
100g/4oz block margarine
Finely grated zest and juice
    of 1 orange
275g/10oz self-raising flour
10g/4oz soft light brown
    sugar
1 egg, beaten
100g/4oz dried, no-soak
    apricots, chopped
25g/1oz dried cranberries

Topping:

100g/4oz icing sugar
4 tsp fresh orange juice
25g/1oz each chopped
    apricots and cranberries
    to decorate

1 Preheat the oven to 180°C/350°F/Gas 4. Grease and line the base of a 450g/1lb loaf tin.

2 Melt the marmalade with the margarine over a low heat, stirring until the fat melts. Remove from the heat and add the orange juice and zest. Cool for 5 minutes.

3 Place all the remaining ingredients except the fruit in a bowl and add the melted mixture. Beat together until smooth, then fold in the fruit.

Spoon into the tin and bake for 40 minutes until risen and firm in the centre.

4 Cool in the tin for 5 minutes, then turn out to cool and peel away the lining paper.

5 To make the topping, blend the icing sugar with the orange juice to make a smooth, runny icing. Drizzle over the top of the cake, then scatter the centre with chopped apricots and cranberries.

Cook's tip:

Cool the cake and freeze undecorated for up to 3 months. Thaw at room temperature, then decorate with icing as above.

Mincemeat Cake

Party Special

Make this cake with ingredients from the store cupboard. It is a great last-minute cake for celebrations, such as anniversaries or Christmas, and keeps well for 2 weeks.

Ingredients:

100g/4oz butter
100g/4oz soft dark muscovado sugar
3 eggs, beaten
225g/8oz self-raising flour
1 tsp mixed spice
400g/14oz jar of fruit mincemeat
75g/3oz glacé cherries
75g/3oz no-soak prunes, chopped
50g/2oz walnut pieces, chopped
50g/2oz plain chocolate, grated

Topping:

25g/1oz sieved apricot jam
100g/4oz glacé fruits such as ginger, pineapple, apricots, cherries

35 minutes preparation
1 hour 45 minutes baking
Serves 12

1 Preheat the oven to 160°C/325°F/Gas 3. Grease and double line the base and sides of a 20cm/ 8 inch round, deep cake tin with non-stick paper.

2 Beat the butter and sugar together until light and fluffy, then add the egg a little at a time, using a little flour with each addition.

3 Sift the remaining flour and spice into the bowl, then fold in with all the remaining ingredients. Spoon into the tin, make a slight hollow in the centre, then spread the sides level.

4 Bake in the centre of the oven for 1 hour 45 minutes to 2 hours. Test with a skewer – if it comes out cleanly, the cake is done. Cool the cake in the tin.

5 For the topping, brush the cake top with apricot glaze, place the glacé fruits on top in an attractive pattern, and brush again with glaze.

Simnel Cake

Family Favourite

Traditionally, Simnel cake was made for Mothering Sunday, but it has now become a popular treat for Easter. Let the children add their own decorations, such as mini Easter eggs and chicks.

45 minutes preparation
2 hours baking
Serves 10

Ingredients:

225g/8oz plain flour
1 tsp baking powder
2 tsp mixed spice
175g/6oz butter, softened
175g/6oz light soft brown
    sugar
3 large eggs
450g/1lb mixed dried fruit

50g/2oz glacé cherries,
    rinsed, halved
2 tbsp milk
Finely grated zest of 1
    lemon
450g/1lb almond paste
2 tbsp sieved apricot jam

1 Preheat the oven to 160°C/350°F/Gas 3. Grease and line an 18cm/ 7 inch round, deep cake tin with non-stick baking paper.

2 Sift the flour, baking powder and spice together. Beat the butter with the sugar until light and fluffy, then gradually beat in the eggs one at a time, adding a little flour with each addition.

3 Add the fruit, milk, remaining flour and lemon zest and stir until evenly combined. Roll out one-third of the almond paste to a disc the same size as the tin. Place half the cake mixture in the tin and put the almond paste disc on top. Cover with the remainder of the cake mixture and smooth the top level. Bake for 2 hours or until the centre is firm. Stand the cake in the tin for 5 minutes, then turn out to cool on a wire rack. When cold, brush the top with apricot glaze.

4 Roll out half the remaining almond paste to a round big enough to fit the top. Place on the cake and mark a criss-cross pattern on top and make a fluted edge. Roll the remaining paste into eleven balls and arrange on top of the cake in a ring. Toast the top of the cake lightly to make the tops of the balls light golden.

sponges and light cakes

Cappuccino Coffee Cake

Quick and Easy

If you love coffee, then you'll really enjoy this light, fluffy cake. For a touch of extra luxury, try using a coffee liqueur, such as Tia Maria or Kaluha, instead of coffee essence.

Ingredients:

1 tsp instant coffee granules
150g/5oz self-raising flour
25g/1oz cocoa powder
1 tsp baking powder
175g/6oz soft-tub margarine
175g/6oz caster sugar
3 eggs

Filling and Topping:

300ml/¹/₂pt double cream
1 tbsp coffee essence
1 tbsp icing sugar
2 tbsp chocolate sprinkles
   or cocoa

20 minutes preparation
20 minutes baking
Serves 8

1 Preheat the oven to 190°C/375°F/Gas 5. Grease two 20cm/8 inch sandwich tins and line the bases with non-stick baking paper. Dissolve the coffee in 1 tablespoon of boiling water and cool.

2 Sift the flour, cocoa and baking powder into a large bowl. Add the margarine, sugar, eggs and cold coffee. Beat together for about 2 minutes until the mixture is smooth.

3 Spoon into the tins and spread level. Bake for 20 minutes, or until risen and firm in the middle. Turn out to cool on a wire rack.

4 To make the filling and topping, whisk the cream until it forms soft peaks, then fold in the icing sugar and essence.

5 Spread half over the top of one cake and place the other layer on top. Spread with the remaining cream and scatter the chocolate sprinkles or cocoa on top just before serving.

Lemon Drizzle Squares

Family Favourite

These little sponge squares are light and refreshing, and the lemon syrup keeps them wonderfully moist.

Ingredients:

175g/6oz butter or block margarine, softened
175g/6oz caster sugar
3 eggs, beaten
175g/6oz self-raising flour
2 small lemons

Topping:

50g/2oz caster sugar
1 small lemon

15 minutes preparation
35 minutes baking
Serves 9

1 Preheat the oven to 180°C/350°F/Gas 4. Grease an 18cm/7 inch square cake tin and line the base with non-stick baking paper.

2 Place the butter or margarine and sugar in a bowl. Add the eggs and sift in the flour. Finely grate the zest from the 2 lemons into the bowl.

3 Beat together for about 2 minutes until the mixture is light and fluffy. Spoon into the tin and spread level. Bake for about 35-40 minutes until firm and golden. Cool in the tin.

4 To make the topping, cut the zest from the lemon into thin strips and put to one side. Squeeze the juice from the lemon into a small pan. Add the sugar and warm until it dissolves, then add the strips of zest and cool slightly. Spoon the syrup and the zest over the cake while still warm. Scatter with a little extra caster sugar and cut into 9 squares.

Cook's tip:

To freeze, cool the cake, top with the syrup and freeze in the baking tin wrapped in foil. Keeps for 2 months. To thaw, unwrap, remove from the tin and defrost at room temperature for 2 hours.

Victoria Sandwich

Easy Entertaining

No Sunday afternoon tea would be complete without a proper Victoria sponge. You can make it with just a jam layer or just cream, but I prefer both!

Ingredients:

**225g/8oz soft-tub margarine
  or softened butter
225g/8oz caster sugar
225g/8oz self-raising flour
1 tsp baking powder
4 eggs
1 tbsp milk**

Filling:

**4 tbsp raspberry jam
90ml/3fl oz double cream,
  whipped
Caster or icing sugar for
  dusting**

10 minutes preparation
25 minutes baking
Serves 8

1. Preheat the oven to 180°C/350°F/Gas 4. Grease two 20cm/8 inch sandwich tins and line the bases with non-stick baking paper.

2. Place all the ingredients in a large bowl and beat together for 2 minutes until smooth. Divide the mixture between the tins and smooth level.

3. Bake for about 25 minutes or until well-risen and springy in the centre. Cool in the tins for 5 minutes, then turn out to cool on a wire rack. When cold, peel away the papers.

4. For the filling, spread one cake with jam, and the underside of the other with cream. Sandwich together and sift caster or icing sugar over the top.

Cook's tip:

To test if the cakes are baked, press the centre lightly with your finger and the sponge should spring back.

Cherry & Coconut Slice

Family Favourite

It's always handy to have a nice, moist cake in the cake tin. This one is an old favourite, full of sweet coconut flavours and juicy cherries.

Ingredients:

100g/4oz glacé cherries
225g/8oz self-raising flour
175g/6oz softened butter or soft-tub margarine
175g/6oz natural caster sugar
3 eggs
1 tbsp milk
50g/2oz desiccated coconut

15 minutes preparation
50 minutes baking
Serves 8

1 Preheat the oven to 180°C/350°F/Gas 4. Grease and line the base of a 900g/2lb loaf tin with non-stick baking paper.

2 Wash the syrup from the cherries, dry them, then cut them in half. Place the flour, butter and sugar in a bowl with the eggs.

3 Beat the mixture until smooth for about 2 minutes. Fold in the cherries and coconut with the milk.

4 Spoon into the loaf tin and smooth the top level. Bake for 50 minutes until the cake is risen, firm and light golden. Insert a skewer into the middle and ensure it comes out cleanly. Cool in the tin, then turn out to cool on a wire rack.

Cook's tip:

Wrap and freeze the cake whole, or freeze leftover cut slices wrapped in foil for up to 2 months.

Seed Cake

Family Favourite

Moist and spicy seed cake dates back to Victorian times and was popular as a mid-morning delicacy. It was common for your bank manager to offer you a slice with a glass of Madeira. How times have changed!

Ingredients:

175g/6oz butter, softened
175g/6oz caster sugar
3 eggs, beaten
25g/1oz ground almonds
1 tbsp caraway seeds
175g/6oz self-raising flour

15 minutes preparation
40 minutes baking
Serves 8

1 Preheat the oven to 180°C/350°F/Gas 4. Grease and line the base of an 18cm/7 inch round cake tin.

2 Place the butter and sugar in a bowl and beat until light and fluffy. Add the eggs, a little at a time, beating well between each addition.

3 Stir the almonds, caraway seeds and flour together and gently fold into the creamed mixture in the bowl.

4 Spoon into the prepared tin and smooth the top level. Bake for about 40 minutes until a skewer inserted into the centre comes out cleanly. Cool in the tin for 5 minutes then turn out on to a wire rack.

Cook's tip:

Use the back of a wetted tablespoon to smooth the top of the cake mixture as this will slide around with ease.

Easy Orange Sponge

Quick and Easy

This recipe is easy enough for the kids to try. It will always rise well and it doesn't matter if the icing is not perfect. So, encourage them to start baking now.

Ingredients:

1 large orange
175g/6oz self-raising flour
1 tsp baking powder
175g/6oz soft-tub margarine
175g/6oz caster sugar
3 eggs

Filling and Topping:

4 tbsp orange marmalade
Half an orange
100g/4oz icing sugar

15 minutes preparation
20 minutes baking
Serves 8

1 Preheat the oven to 180°C/350°F/Gas 4. Grease and line the bases of two 20cm/8 inch sandwich tins with non-stick baking paper.

2 Finely grate the zest from the orange and squeeze out 1 tablespoon of juice. Sift the flour and baking powder into a bowl and add the orange zest, juice and all the remaining cake ingredients. Beat until smooth, then divide between the tins and smooth level.

3 Bake for 20 minutes until each cake springs back when pressed in the centre is.

Cool in the tins for 5 minutes, then transfer to a wire rack.

4 For the filling and topping, sandwich the cakes together with the marmalade. Cut long thin shreds of zest from half an orange, then squeeze out the juice. Sift the icing sugar into a bowl and add enough juice to make a runny icing. Add a little orange colouring if preferred.

5 Smooth over the top of the cake, allowing some icing to drizzle down the sides. Slice the zest finely and scatter over the top.

Cook's tip:

Make a lemon version by substituting lemon rind and juice for the orange, and sandwiching the cake with lemon curd.

Honey, Ginger & Lemon Gateau

spicy

30 minutes preparation

25 minutes baking

Serves 8

Ingredients:

100g/4oz clear honey
100g/4oz dark treacle
125ml/4fl oz sunflower oil
100g/4oz soft dark
   muscovado sugar
125ml/4fl oz milk
225g/8oz plain flour
1 tsp ground ginger
1 egg
1 tsp bicarbonate of soda
50g/2oz stem ginger,
   drained and chopped

Frosting:

225g/8oz icing sugar
100g/4oz unsalted butter,
   softened
2 lemons
Stem ginger

1 Grease two 20cm/8 inch sandwich tins and line the bases with non-stick baking paper. Preheat the oven to 180°C/350°F/Gas 4.

2 Put the honey, treacle, oil and sugar in a pan and heat gently to dissolve the sugar. Remove from the heat, then stir in the milk.

3 Sift the flour and ginger into a bowl. Stir in the egg. Whisk the bicarbonate of soda into the melted mixture, then beat into the flour with a wooden spoon. Fold in the chopped ginger.

4 Divide between the tins and bake for about 25 minutes, or until the cakes are springy to the touch. Cool in the tins for 5 minutes, then turn out to cool on a wire rack.

5 To make the frosting, sift the icing sugar into a bowl and gradually beat in the butter until fluffy and smooth. Finely grate the rind and squeeze in the juice from one lemon. Beat into the buttercream. Slice the remaining lemon thinly.

6 Use half of the frosting to sandwich the cakes together, then spread half the remainder over the top. Place the remaining cream in a piping bag and pipe stars around the edge of the gateau. Decorate with lemon slices and ginger.

Coconut & Orange Cake

Family Favourite

This variation of carrot cake is coated in fluffy white frosting and sweet coconut strands. The carrots and coconut make it a moist and long-keeping cake.

Ingredients:

225g/8oz butter or block
    margarine
225g/8oz soft light brown
    sugar
4 eggs, beaten
225g/8oz plain flour
2 tsp baking powder
Finely grated rind of 1
    orange
175g/6oz finely grated carrot
50g/2oz desiccated coconut

Frosting:

175g/6oz white vegetable fat
350g/12oz icing sugar, sifted
2-3 tbsp milk
100g/4oz sweetened,
    shredded coconut

30 minutes preparation
1 hour 30 minutes baking
Serves 10

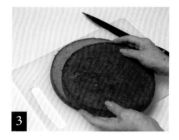

1 Preheat the oven to 180°C/350°F/Gas 4. Grease a 20cm/8 inch round, loose-based cake tin and line the base with non-stick baking paper.

2 Beat the fat and sugar together until pale and fluffy. Gradually beat in the eggs, adding a teaspoon of flour with each addition.

3 Sift in the flour and baking powder and fold in with the carrot and coconut. Spoon into the tin and make a hollow in the centre. Bake for about

1 hour 30 minutes, or until well-risen and firm in the centre. Cool on a wire rack. Cut the cake in half horizontally.

4 To make the frosting, put the white fat and the icing sugar in a bowl and beat together with the milk.

5 Spread over the top and sides of the cake. Sprinkle with the sweetened coconut and place on a serving plate.

Swiss Roll

No-fat cake

A Swiss roll is such a handy cake – make it from store cupboard ingredients in a morning ready for afternoon visitors. It contains no fat at all, so you can go mad and serve it with lashings of clotted cream and strawberries.

Ingredients:

3 large eggs
100g/4oz caster sugar
100g/4oz plain flour
6 tbsp seedless raspberry jam, warmed
Icing sugar to dredge

20 minutes preparation
10 minutes baking
Serves 8

1 Preheat the oven to 200°C/400°F/Gas 6. Grease and line a 33x23cm/13x9 inch Swiss roll tin with a sheet of non-stick baking paper, 5cm/2 inches larger than the tin. Snip the corners to fit.

2 Place the eggs and caster sugar in a heatproof bowl and set over a pan of hot water. Whisk with an electric mixer until very thick and pale. The mixer should leave a trail when the beaters are lifted away. Remove from the pan and whisk until cold and thick.

3 Sift half the flour into the mixture and fold in carefully. Sift in the remaining flour and fold in with 1 tablespoon of warm water. Spread into the tin and smooth level into all the corners. Bake for 10 minutes,

or until golden and firm to the touch.

4 While the sponge is baking, spread a dampened tea towel on a flat surface, lay a large sheet of non-stick paper on top of this and sprinkle with caster sugar. Turn the cooked sponge out on to the sugared paper and trim away the crusty edges. Spread with the warmed jam.

5 Roll up the sponge, using the paper as a guide. Leave the cake to cool wrapped up in the paper to prevent it from unrolling. To serve, remove the paper and dust with icing sugar.

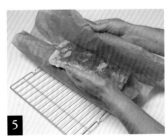

Orange Marble Cake

Easy Entertaining

This cake always looks impressive, but it really is quite simple to make. If you don't have a ring mould tin, use a 20cm/8 inch round cake tin instead.

Ingredients:

225g/8oz soft-tub margarine
225g/8oz golden caster sugar
4 eggs
225g/8oz self-raising flour
50g/2oz plain chocolate,
  melted
Finely grated zest and juice
  of 1 orange

Icing:

175g/6oz plain chocolate
100g/4oz unsalted butter
50g/2oz white chocolate,
  melted

1 hour preparation
50 minutes baking
Serves 8

1 Preheat the oven to 180°C/350°F/Gas 4. Grease a 1.7l/3 pint ring mould, then line with thin strips of non-stick paper.

2 Place the margarine, sugar, eggs and flour in a bowl and beat together for about 2 minutes until smooth. Place half the mixture in a separate bowl and stir in the melted chocolate. Add the orange zest and juice to the other half.

3 Place alternate tablespoonfuls of the mixture in the tin and draw a knife through them to create a marbled effect. Bake for 50 minutes, or until a warmed skewer inserted into the centre, comes out cleanly.

4 Cool in the tin for 5 minutes then turn out on to a wire rack and lift away the ring mould.

5 To make the icing, break the chocolate into pieces and place in a bowl with the butter and 2 tablespoons of water. Place over a pan of warm water, or in the microwave, and melt together, stirring occasionally.

6 Pour the icing over the cake, spreading it evenly around the top and sides. Leave it to set for 30 minutes. Place the white chocolate in a small paper icing bag, snip away the end and drizzle over the top.

chocolate cakes

Chocolate Fudge Cake

Easy Entertaining

Ingredients:

3 tbsp cocoa powder
175g/6oz plain flour
2 tsp baking powder
175g/6oz butter, softened
1 tsp vanilla essence
225g/8oz golden caster sugar
3 eggs, beaten
100g/4oz plain chocolate,
   melted
150ml/¼ pint soured cream

Fudge Frosting:

225g/8oz plain chocolate
250ml/9fl oz double cream
Fresh strawberries to
   decorate

30 minutes preparation
50 minutes baking
Serves 8-10

1 Preheat the oven to 180°C/350°F/Gas 4. Grease and line the base and sides of a deep 20cm/8 inch round cake tin. Blend the cocoa to a paste with 4 tablespoons of boiling water. Sift the flour and baking powder together.

2 Beat the butter, vanilla and sugar together in a large bowl until light and fluffy. Gradually beat in the eggs a little at a time. Fold in the flour with the cocoa mixture, melted chocolate and soured cream.

3 Spoon the mixture into the tin and smooth it level. Make a slight hollow in the centre to stop the cake from peaking. Bake for 50-55 minutes until a skewer inserted into the centre comes out

cleanly. Cool in the tin for 5 minutes, then move to a wire rack. When cold, cut in half horizontally.

4 To make the frosting, break up the chocolate and melt in a bowl over warm water, or in the microwave. Stir in the cream, beat until smooth, then cool. Whisk the icing with an electric mixer until fluffy and light, chill for 15 minutes, then whisk again.

5 Spread a little icing on one cake half, then sandwich the cake together. Spread the frosting over the top and sides of the cake. Decorate with strawberries to serve. Keep the cake refrigerated until needed.

Brownies

Freezer Friendly

Brownies keep well in an airtight tin for 4-5 days, but they do have a habit of disappearing – how long will they stay around in your house?

Ingredients:

100g/4oz butter or block margarine
1 tbsp cocoa powder
50g/2oz plain chocolate
175g/6oz dark muscovado sugar
2 eggs, beaten
150g/5oz self-raising flour
100g/5oz walnut pieces, chopped

15 minutes preparation
35 minutes baking
Makes 12 squares

1 Preheat the oven to 180°C/350°F/Gas 4. Grease and line the base of a 20cm/8 inch shallow square cake tin with non-stick paper. Melt 50g/2oz of the butter with the cocoa and then add the chocolate broken into pieces.

2 Remove from the heat and stir until the chocolate has melted, then put aside to cool. Beat the remaining butter with the sugar until light and fluffy.

3 Gradually beat in the eggs, then fold in the flour, nuts and the cooled, melted mixture.

4 Spoon into the tin and spread the top level. Bake for about 35 minutes until firm to the touch in the centre.

5 Cool in the tin, then turn out. Peel away the lining paper and cut into 12 small squares.

Cook's tip:

To freeze, wrap the uncut block of cake tightly in foil and freeze. Keeps for 3 months.

Choc Chip Banana Loaf

Family Favourite

There's not too much washing up to do when you make this cake – it's all mixed together in a saucepan.

Ingredients:

20 minutes preparation
40-50 minutes baking
Serves 8

175g/6oz block margarine
225g/8oz golden caster sugar
275g/10oz ripe bananas (before peeling)
1 tsp vanilla essence
275g/10oz self-raising flour
1 tsp bicarbonate of soda
3 eggs, beaten
100g/4oz milk chocolate chips

1 Preheat the oven to 180°C/350°F/Gas 4. Grease and line a 900g/2lb loaf tin.

2 Heat the margarine and sugar in a saucepan over a low heat until the sugar dissolves. Remove from the heat and cool for 5 minutes.

3 Peel and mash the bananas together with the vanilla essence. Sift the flour and bicarbonate of soda into the pan with the melted mixture, then beat in the eggs and mashed bananas.

4 Fold in the chocolate chips, then spoon into the tin. Bake for 40-50 minutes or until a skewer inserted into the centre of the cake comes out cleanly. Leave to stand in the tin for 5 minutes then turn out to cool on a wire rack. When cold, wrap in foil until needed.

Cook's tip:

The cake will form a crack across the top as it rises during baking, but don't worry, this is normal.

Chocolate Scone Round

Quick and Easy

This fluffy chocolate scone is made in just minutes and sandwiched together with a tangy, orange-flavoured buttercream. It's ideal for adding to lunch boxes.

Ingredients:

2 tbsp cocoa powder
225g/8oz plain flour
2 tsp baking powder
75g/3oz butter or block
**   margarine, diced**
75g/3oz soft dark brown sugar
5 tbsp milk
1 egg

Filling:

1 large orange
50g/2oz unsalted butter,
**   softened**
100g/4oz icing sugar
Orange food colouring

10 minutes preparation
15 minutes baking
Serves 8

1 Preheat the oven to 220°C/425°F/Gas 7. Lightly grease a baking sheet. Sift the cocoa, flour and baking powder together into a bowl.

2 Add the fat to the bowl and rub in with your fingertips until the mixture resembles fine crumbs. Stir in the sugar. Beat the egg with the milk. Pour into the bowl and mix to a soft dough.

3 Turn the dough on to a lightly floured surface and knead until smooth. Roll out to a 20cm/8 inch circle and place on the baking sheet. Mark into 8 wedges and bake for 15

minutes until risen and firm. Lift the scone round on to a wire rack to cool.

4 To make the filling, grate the rind from the orange and squeeze out the juice. Beat the butter with the icing sugar and mix in 3 tablespoons of juice and the rind. Add a little orange food colouring and beat until smooth.

5 Separate the scones and split each one in half. Spread with orange buttercream and sift a little icing sugar over the top of each one.

Chocolate Drop Cup Cake

Quick and Easy

These chocolate cup cakes are quick and easy to make. Let the children help to make and decorate them.

Ingredients:

100g/4oz butter, softened
100g/4oz soft light brown
   sugar
2 eggs
100g/4oz self-raising flour
25g/1oz cocoa
50g/2oz plain chocolate chips

Icing:

25g/1oz butter, melted
25g/1oz cocoa
1 tbsp milk
100g/4oz golden icing
   sugar
50g/2oz milk chocolate
   mini buttons

25 minutes preparation
15 minutes baking
Makes 18

1 Preheat the oven to 190°C/375°F/Gas 5. Line 18 bun tins with foil or paper cases.

2 Sift the flour and cocoa into a bowl. Add the butter, sugar and eggs. Beat until smooth, then stir in the chocolate chips.

3 Divide the mixture between the lined bun cases. Bake in the centre of the oven for about 15 minutes, until the buns spring back when lightly pressed. Remove the buns to a wire rack to cool.

4 To make the icing, beat the butter with the cocoa, milk and icing sugar until smooth.

5 Spread over the tops of the buns and sprinkle each one with a few chocolate buttons. Leave to set for 30 minutes before serving.

Cook's tip:

Fill the paper cases only two-thirds full to allow the cakes to rise in a neat shape.

Classic Chocolate Profiteroles

Easy Entertaining

Profiteroles make an easy supper-party dessert. I always bake the bases well ahead of time and store them in a tin, then all you need to do is fill them with cream and drizzle chocolate sauce over them just before serving.

Ingredients:

50g/2oz butter
60g/2½oz plain flour, sifted
A pinch of salt
2 eggs, beaten

Filling and Topping:

300ml/½ pint double cream, whipped
200g/7oz plain chocolate, melted

35 minutes preparation
20 minutes baking
Makes 18

1 Preheat the oven to 200°C/400°F/Gas 6. Grease two baking sheets. Place 150ml/¼ pint water in a heavy-based pan. Add the butter and bring to the boil.

2 Remove from the heat. Add the flour all at once and beat with a wooden spoon until a soft ball forms. Cool slightly, then whisk in the eggs, a little at a time, with an electric mixer, until the mixture is smooth and glossy.

3 Place 18 teaspoons of the mixture on to the sheets. Bake for 10 minutes, then increase the temperature to 220°C/425°F/Gas 7 and bake for a further 10-15 minutes until crisp and golden. Remove to a wire rack and slit one side of each bun to allow any steam to escape then cool completely.

4 For the filling and topping, spoon the whipped cream into each bun, close the tops, then dip each top in the melted chocolate and serve at once.

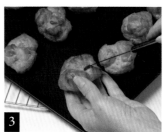

Cook's tip:

Sprinkle a little water over the baking sheet after greasing, as this produces steam in the oven and helps the buns to rise.

Carob Cake

Something Special

One of our friends can't eat chocolate as it gives her headaches, so I make this cake using carob which tastes just as chocolately. You'll find it on sale in health-food shops.

Ingredients:

2 tbsp carob powder
225g/8oz soft-tub margarine
225g/8oz soft dark brown sugar
4 eggs
1 tsp vanilla essence
225g/8oz self-raising flour

Filling:

425g/15oz can crushed pineapple
225g/8oz full-fat cream cheese
1 tbsp caster sugar
225g/8oz fromage frais
75g/3oz carob bar

50 minutes preparation
30 minutes baking
Serves 8

1 Preheat the oven to 180°C/35°F/Gas 4. Grease and line the bases of two 20cm/8 inch round sandwich tins. Mix the carob powder to a paste with 4 tablespoons of cold water.

2 Place all the remaining cake ingredients into a large bowl and add the carob paste. Beat together for about 2 minutes until light and fluffy. Spread into the tins and make a slight hollow in the centres.

3 Bake for 30-35 minutes until springy in the centres. Cool in the tins for 10 minutes, then cool on a rack.

4 To make the filling, drain the pineapple in a sieve and chop finely if there are any large pieces. Soften the cream cheese in a bowl, fold in the fromage frais and the sugar, then stir in the pineapple.

5 Sandwich the cake together with one-third of the filling, then spread the remainder over the top and sides. Grate the carob bar into large flakes and sprinkle over the cake.

Chocolate & Almond Slice

Freezer Friendly

This supermoist slice is simply packed with chocolate and covered in a squidgy chocolate spread.

Ingredients:

225g/8oz dark plain chocolate, broken into pieces
225g/8oz butter
5 eggs
50g/2oz golden caster sugar
100g/4oz self-raising flour
75g/3oz ground almonds

Icing and Filling:

300ml/½ pint double cream
150g/5oz plain dark chocolate, broken into pieces
A few drops of almond essence
Chocolate flakes to decorate

1 hour preparation
35 minutes baking
Serves 8

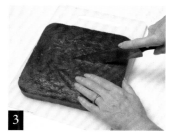

1 Preheat the oven to 160°C/325°F/Gas 3. Grease and line the base of a 23cm/9 inch square cake tin with non-stick baking paper.

2 Place the chocolate in a bowl and add the butter cut into small chunks. Melt over a pan of warm water, or in the microwave on Low. Whisk the eggs and sugar together until thick. Sift the flour into the mixture and fold in with the ground almonds and the melted mixture.

3 Pour into the tin and bake for 35 minutes until firm and risen. Cool in the tin for 5 minutes, then turn out to cool on a wire rack. Trim the cake and cut in half.

4 To make the filling, heat half the cream until almost boiling, remove from the heat and add the chocolate pieces. Stir until the chocolate melts, then pour into a bowl and beat until cool and thick.

5 Whip the remaining cream with the almond essence and use to sandwich the cake together.

6 Spread the chocolate cream over the top and sides with a palette knife and decorate the top with chocolate curls.

Devil's Food Cake

Easy Entertaining

The beauty of the frosting on this dark, chocolate sponge is that it takes only seven minutes to whip up. You'll need to swirl it on straight away as it sets quickly.

Ingredients:

175g/6oz plain flour
1 tsp baking powder
½ tsp bicarbonate of soda
50g/2oz cocoa powder
100g/4oz butter, softened
225g/8oz soft dark brown
    sugar
2 eggs, beaten
4 tbsp soured cream

Frosting:

2 large egg whites
350g/12 oz caster sugar
Pinch of salt
Pinch of cream of tartar

50 minutes preparation
35 minutes baking
Serves 10

1 Preheat the oven to 190°C/350°F/Gas 5. Grease and line the bases of two 20cm/8 inch round sandwich tins.

2 Sift the flour, baking powder and bicarbonate of soda together. Mix the cocoa to a smooth paste, with 3 tablespoons of boiling water. Beat the butter and sugar together until light and fluffy.

3 Whisk in the eggs, soured cream and the cocoa mixture, then fold in the sifted flour and stir until smooth. Divide between the tins and smooth level. Bake for 35 minutes until firm to the touch. Cool for 5 minutes then turn out to cool on a wire rack.

4 To make the frosting, place the egg whites, sugar, salt, cream of tartar and 1 tablespoon of warm water in a large heatproof bowl. Place the bowl over a pan of hot water and whisk, using an electric whisk for 7 minutes until the mixture is thick and white and stands in peaks.

5 Sandwich the cakes together with the frosting. Place the cake on a serving dish and swirl over the top and sides with a palette knife.

Chocolate & Strawberry Roulade

Party Special

I always make the base for this dessert cake the evening before I need it. It will become moist and squidgy overnight, and all you need to do is to fill it with cream and fruit before you serve it.

Ingredients:

2 tsp instant coffee granules
100g/4oz plain chocolate,
**   melted**
4 large eggs, separated
100g/4oz caster sugar

Filling:

300ml/¹/₂ pint whipping
**   cream**
100g/4oz strawberries,
sliced
Icing sugar for dusting

30 minutes preparation
15 minutes baking
Serves 6-8

1 Preheat the oven to 180°C/350°F/Gas 4. Grease and line a 28x33cm/11x13 inch Swiss roll tin with non-stick baking paper. Blend the coffee to a smooth paste with 1 tablespoon of warm water.

2 Whisk the egg yolks and sugar together in a bowl over a pan of hot water until thick and pale. Remove from the heat and stir in the cooled, melted chocolate and coffee mixture.

3 Whisk the egg whites until stiff, then fold 3 tablespoons into the chocolate mixture to loosen it. Fold in the remaining egg whites carefully.

4 Spread the mixture into the tin and bake for about 15 minutes until the top is firm. Cool in the tin on a wire rack. Sprinkle a large sheet of greaseproof paper with icing sugar and turn the cake out on to it. Peel away the lining paper and trim away the crusty edges of the cake.

5 For the filling, spread the roulade with cream and sliced strawberries and roll up the cake using the paper to help guide it. Serve sifted with icing sugar.

Cook's tip:

Roulades do tend to crack when rolled up, but don't worry, this just adds to their appeal!

wholewheat
bakes

Date Slices

Freezer Friendly

The evaporated milk in these chewy bars, combined with sticky dates, gives them a delicious toffee flavour.

Ingredients:

200ml/7fl oz evaporated milk
175g/6oz stoned, dried dates, chopped
100g/4oz butter or block margarine
75g/3oz golden caster sugar
1 tsp vanilla essence
50g/2oz wholewheat flour
150g/5oz self-raising flour
50g/2oz walnuts, chopped
1 tbsp golden icing sugar

20 minutes preparation
25 minutes baking
Makes 12 slices

1 Preheat the oven to 180°C/350°F/Gas 4. Grease and line the base of an 18x27cm/7x11 inch shallow tin. Place the evaporated milk and dates into a pan and cook over a low heat until just boiling, stirring well.

2 Pour the mixture into a bowl and mash the dates with a fork until the mixture is thick and sticky. Leave to cool for 15 minutes.

3 Meanwhile, beat the butter, sugar and vanilla essence together in a large bowl, until light and fluffy. Stir in the cooled date mixture and the flours, then stir in the chopped nuts. Spoon into the tin and spread level.

4 Bake for 25 minutes until firm and risen, then cool in the tin for 5 minutes. Turn out of the tin to cool on a wire rack. Dust with icing sugar and cut into 12 slices with a sharp knife.

Cook's tip:

Freeze the cooled cake without the icing sugar topping. Wrap in foil and freeze for up to 2 months.

Blue Cheese & Broccoli Tart

vegetarian

If you have a vegetarian to feed, this is a recipe that all the family can enjoy as well.

Pastry:

175g/6oz wholewheat flour
75g/3oz vegetable margarine
25g/1oz Parmesan cheese, finely grated

Filling:

225g/8oz small broccoli florets
100g/4oz carrots, thinly sliced
100g/4oz blue cheese, crumbled
50g/2oz mixed chopped nuts
3 eggs
225ml/8fl oz milk

30 minutes preparation
30 minutes baking
Serves 6-8

1 Preheat the oven to 200°C/400°F/Gas 6. Grease a 23cm/9 inch fluted flan dish and place on a baking sheet. To make the pastry, place the flour in a bowl with the margarine and rub in until the mixture resembles fine crumbs. Stir in the grated Parmesan and about 2 tablespoons of cold water. Mix to a soft dough then wrap and chill for 5 minutes.

2 Cook the carrots in boiling salted water for 5 minutes and the broccoli for 2 minutes. Drain and refresh under cold running water.

3 Roll out the pastry to a circle large enough to line the flan dish. Prick the base with a fork, fill with greaseproof paper and baking beans. Bake blind for 15 minutes. Remove the paper and beans and bake for another 5 minutes.

4 Layer the carrots and broccoli in the case. Scatter the cheese over the top. Beat the eggs and milk together and pour into the flan. Top with the nuts and bake for about 30 minutes until golden and firm in the centre. Serve hot or cold.

Wholewheat Carrot Cake

Freezer Friendly

There are many versions of carrot cake, or Passion cake as it is sometimes known. I like to use wholewheat flour for this spicy cake as it helps to give it an extra moist texture.

Ingredients:

225g/8oz carrot
225g/8oz soft-tub margarine
225g/8oz soft light brown sugar
4 eggs, beaten
225g/8oz wholewheat flour
2 tsp baking powder
1 tsp ground cinnamon
50g/2oz ground hazelnuts
75g/3oz sultanas
2 tbsp milk

Frosting:

175g/6oz full-fat, soft cream cheese
175g/6oz natural icing sugar
1 tsp lemon juice

30 minutes preparation
1 hour 15 minutes baking
Serves 12

1. Preheat the oven to 180°C/350°F/Gas 4. Grease and line the base of a 20cm/8 inch round, spring-clipped cake tin with non-stick baking paper. Peel and finely grate the carrots.

2. Place the margarine, sugar and eggs in a bowl and sift in the flour, cinnamon and baking powder, adding any bran from the sieve.

3. Beat for 2 minutes, then stir in the carrot, hazelnuts and sultanas with enough milk to make a soft mixture. Spoon into the tin and make a hollow in the centre of the cake with the back of a metal spoon.

4. Bake for 1 hour 15 minutes, or until well-risen and firm to the touch. Cool in the tin for 10 minutes, then turn out to cool on a wire rack. To make the frosting, beat the cream cheese, icing sugar and lemon juice together.

5. Spread the frosting over the top and sides of the cake in large swirls.

Ginger Parkin

spicy

Spicy gingerbread is always a family favourite. Unlike other cakes, it does not dry out or go stale quickly, and it will become stickier the longer it is stored in the cake tin.

Ingredients:

150g/5oz plain wholewheat flour
A pinch of salt
1 tsp ground ginger
1 tsp ground cinnamon
2 tsp baking powder
150g/5oz porridge oats
175g/6oz dark muscovado sugar
6 tbsp dark treacle
100g/4oz block margarine
1 egg, beaten
300ml/½pt milk
100g/4oz raisins

20 minutes preparation
1 hour 15 minutes baking
Makes 16 slices

1 Preheat the oven to 180°C/350°F/Gas 4. Grease and line the base of a 23cm/9 inch square cake tin.

2 Sift the flour, salt, spices and baking powder into a large bowl and stir in the oats and sugar.

3 Gently warm the treacle and margarine together in a saucepan, until the fat has melted. Cool slightly.

4 Add to the flour mixture with the egg and milk. Add the raisins and mix together until smooth. The mixture will be very wet. Pour into the tin and bake in the centre of the oven for about 1 hour 15 minutes, or until firm to the touch in the centre.

5 Cool in the tin for 5 minutes, then turn out to cool on a wire rack. Peel away the lining papers while still warm.

6 When completely cold, store the gingerbread in an airtight tin for 2 days to improve the flavour and texture. To serve, cut into 16 slices.

Date & Walnut Teabread

Freezer Friendly

This plain, fruity teabread is delicious served sliced and buttered.

Ingredients:

100g/4oz dried, stoned black dates
50g/2oz walnut pieces
225g/8oz plain wholewheat flour
1 tsp baking powder
75g/3oz soft-tub margarine
75g/3oz soft dark brown sugar
1 tbsp golden syrup
2 eggs, beaten
2 tbsp milk

Glaze:

3 tbsp golden syrup or clear honey

20 minutes preparation
40 minutes baking
Serves 8

1 Preheat the oven to 190°C/375°F/Gas 5. Grease a 900g/2lb loaf tin and line the base with a strip of non-stick baking paper.
Chop the dates finely, then chop the walnut pieces into large chunks.

2 Place all the cake ingredients in a large bowl and beat them together with a wooden spoon for about 2 minutes, until smooth.

If the mixture is dry, add a little more milk.

3 Spoon into the tin and bake for 40 minutes, or until a skewer inserted into the centre comes out cleanly.

4 Cool in the tin for 5 minutes, then turn out on to a wire rack. While the cake is still warm, brush with warmed syrup or honey to glaze the cake.

Cook's tip:

To freeze, cool and wrap in foil. Keeps frozen for up to 3 months.

Oatcakes

Quick and Easy

Crunchy oatcakes are the ideal partner to cheeses. You can buy commercially made ones, but these homemade ones have a lovely nutty flavour and a crunchy and crumbly texture.

Ingredients:

100g/4oz plain flour
1/2 tsp salt
2 tsp baking powder
225g/8oz medium oatmeal
2 tsp caster sugar
75g/3oz margarine
3 tbsp cold water

15 minutes preparation
15 minutes baking
Makes 28 rounds or 16 quartered circles

1 Preheat the oven to 180°C/350°F/Gas 4. Grease two baking sheets. Sift the flour, salt and baking powder into a bowl and stir in the oatmeal and sugar. Add the margarine and rub into the dry ingredients until the mixture resembles coarse crumbs.

2 Add enough water to make a dough of a firm consistency. Knead lightly on a surface sprinkled with flour.

3 Roll out to 6mm/1/4 inch thickness and cut into rounds with a 5cm/2 inch round cutter. Alternatively, cut into 15cm/6 inch circles and then cut the circles into four quarters.

4 Bake for 15 minutes until light golden. Cool on the trays until firm, then lift off with a palette knife and cool on wire racks.

Cook's tip:

When stored in an airtight tin, the oatcakes will keep for up to 2 weeks. Freeze for up to 2 months. If the oatcakes start to become soft, crisp them up under a foil-lined hot grill for a few minutes before serving. Serve with cheese and butter.

Lemon Fig Rolls

Family Favourite

These sticky fig rolls are full of natural, wholewheat goodness. The pastry is crisp and crunchy, the filling sticky and gooey with a hint of lemon.

Ingredients:

150g/5oz soft-tub margarine
175g/6oz golden caster
   sugar
1 egg
275g/10oz plain wholewheat
   flour
1/2 tsp bicarbonate of soda
Finely grated rind of 1 lemon

Filling:

1 lemon
225g/8oz dried figs, chopped
75g/3oz demerara sugar

40 minutes preparation
20 minutes baking
Makes 24

1 To make the pastry, beat the margarine and sugar together, then blend in the egg, flour, bicarbonate and lemon rind with a fork. Form into a ball, wrap in clingfilm and chill for 30 minutes.

2 To make the filling, finely grate the zest from the lemon and squeeze out the juice. Place in a pan with the figs, sugar and 150ml/1/4pt water. Simmer for 20-30 minutes, until the mixture is thick and sticky. Cool.

3 Preheat the oven to 190°C/375°F/Gas 5. Grease two baking sheets. Divide the dough into four pieces and roll each into a rectangle 10x20

cm/4x8 inches. Divide the fig paste into four. Shape each piece into a 20cm/8 inch strip and lay down the centre of each rectangle.

4 Dampen the seam side with a little water. Bring the pastry up over the fig paste to enclose it. Place seam side underneath. Cut each roll in half to form 8 rolls and place on a baking sheet.

5 Bake the rolls in the centre of the oven for 15-20 minutes until firm and browned. Cool slightly, then cut each roll in three with a sharp knife while still warm, then cool on a wire rack.

Mini Pizzas

vegetarian

These pizzas are handy for a quick summer lunch in the garden, or for a children's tea. The uncooked dough can be made ahead and keeps in the freezer for up to 2 months.

Ingredients:

650g/1lb 7oz strong
   wholemeal flour
1 tsp salt
1x7g sachet easy-blend
   yeast
1 tsp soft dark brown sugar
2 tbsp vegetable oil
370ml/12fl oz lukewarm water

Topping:

350g/12 jar chunky tomato
   pizza sauce
2 peppers, sliced
225g/8oz button
   mushrooms, sliced
275g/10oz mozzarella
   cheese, thinly sliced

1 hour preparation
20 minutes baking
Makes 8

1 Mix the flour, salt, sugar and yeast powder together. Whisk the oil and water together and stir into the flour. Mix to a soft dough, turn on to a floured surface and knead for 10 minutes until smooth.

2 Return to the bowl. Cover with oiled clingfilm and leave until doubled in size, for about 30 minutes. Turn out and punch the air out of the dough. Cut into eight equal pieces and roll each one into a ball.

3 Preheat the oven to 220°C/425°F/Gas 7. Grease two baking sheets. Roll each ball to a 12.5cm/5 inch circle and place on the baking sheets.

4 Spread each pizza base with 3 tablespoons of tomato sauce. Scatter the sliced peppers and the sliced mushrooms over the sauce, then top each with the sliced mozzarella cheese.

5 Leave for 15 minutes until the bases are puffy, then bake for 20 minutes until the bases are crisp and the topping golden and bubbling. Serve immediately.

Vegetarian Scone Bake

vegetarian

35 minutes preparation
25 minutes baking
Serves 4

Cheese Sauce:

15g/¹/₂oz vegetable margarine
15g/¹/₂oz plain flour
300ml/¹/₂ pt milk
75g/3oz Cheddar cheese,
    finely grated

Filling:

225g/8oz celery, thinly sliced
225g/8oz carrots, thinly sliced
100g/4oz button mushrooms,
    quartered
400g/14oz can cannelloni
    beans, drained

Topping:

225g/8oz wholewheat flour
2 tsp baking powder
¹/₂ tsp bicarbonate of soda
A pinch of salt
75g/3oz vegetable
    margarine
150ml/¹/₄pt milk
3 tbsp plain yogurt

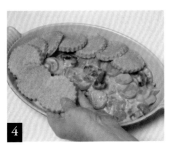

1 To make the sauce, melt the fat in a saucepan and stir in the flour. Cook for 1 minute over a gentle heat. Gradually whisk in the milk and bring to the boil, stirring all the time. Simmer for 3 minutes, then add the cheese and stir until melted and blended.

2 Preheat the oven to 200°C/400°F/Gas 6. Grease a shallow 2l/3¹/₄pt ovenproof dish. Add the sliced vegetables and beans to the sauce and spoon into the base of the dish.

3 To make the topping, sift the flour with the baking powder, bicarbonate and salt.

Add the margarine, cut into small pieces and rub into the flour until the mixture resembles fine crumbs. Stir in the milk and yogurt to make a soft dough and knead until smooth.

4 Roll out the dough and cut out 12 rounds with a 6cm/2 ¹/₂ inch round cutter. Place the rounds on top of the vegetables, overlapping them and leaving the centre open. Brush the scones with a little milk and bake for 20-25 minutes until the scones are risen and golden and the filling is hot and bubbling. Serve immediately.

Soda Bread

Low Fat

If you run out of bread over a busy weekend, don't worry. Just bake this easy, yeast-free bread and serve it within the hour. It is delicious served warm, and is meant to be eaten on the day of baking.

Ingredients:

225g/8oz plain white flour
325g/12oz wholewheat flour
1 tsp salt
1 tsp bicarbonate of soda
1 tbsp baking powder
1 tsp vegetable oil
150ml/¹/₄pt natural yogurt or buttermilk
150ml/¹/₄pt cold water

15 minutes preparation
30 minutes baking
Makes 2 loaves

1 Preheat the oven to 200°C/400°F/Gas 6. Grease a baking sheet and dust it with flour.

2 Sift the flours, salt, bicarbonate of soda and baking powder into a bowl and add the bran from the sieve into the bowl.

3 Mix the oil and yogurt together with a fork and add to the bowl with the water. Mix to a soft dough, then turn out on to a floured surface and knead until smooth.

4 Divide into two pieces and roll each into a ball.

5 With a sharp knife, cut a deep cross in the middle of each round. Place on the baking sheets and dust each one with flour. Bake for 30 minutes until crisp and browned. Cool for 10 minutes, then break the bread into quarters to serve.

small
cakes

Quick Butterfly Cakes

Quick and Easy

These traditional tea-time favourites are easy to make. Get the kids to make them using different coloured icings.

Ingredients:

100g/4oz soft-tub margarine
100g/4oz caster sugar
2 eggs
100g/4oz self-raising flour
1 tsp baking powder
1 tsp vanilla essence

Icing:

100g/4oz unsalted butter, softened
225g/8oz icing sugar, sifted
1/2 tsp vanilla essence
Pink food colouring
Icing sugar for dusting

30 minutes preparation
15-20 minutes baking
Makes 12-14

1 Preheat the oven to 200°C/400°F/Gas 6. Line a bun tray with 12 paper cases.

2 Place all the cake ingredients in a large bowl and beat with an electric mixer for about 2 minutes until smooth. Half fill the paper cases with the mixture.

3 Bake for 15 minutes or until the cakes are risen and golden. Remove from the bun trays and cool on a wire rack.

4 To make the icing, beat together the butter, icing sugar, colouring and essence until smooth.

5 Cut a slice from the top of each cake, then cut in half to form wings. Pipe or spoon on a little buttercream and replace the halves at an angle to form butterfly wings. Dust with icing sugar before serving.

Cook's tip:

Bake the buns and make the buttercream ahead of time and freeze separately. Defrost and decorate when needed.

Cherry Berry Muffins

Quick and Easy

If you have weekend visitors, make and serve these muffins for breakfast. They are at their best when eaten warm straight from the oven.

Ingredients:

225g/8 oz plain flour
1 tsp baking powder
1/2 tsp bicarbonate of soda
60g/2¹/₂oz caster sugar
1 egg
250ml/8fl oz milk
50g/2oz butter, melted and cooled
50g/2oz red glacé cherries, washed and quartered
75g/3oz raspberries, part thawed if frozen
50g/2oz dried cranberries
Finely grated rind of ¹/₂ orange or lemon

10 minutes preparation
20 minutes baking
Makes 10

1 Preheat the oven to 200°C/400°F/Gas 6. Place 10 large paper muffin cases in deep muffin tins.

2 Sift all the dry ingredients into a bowl and make a well in the centre. Beat the egg and milk together and add to the dry ingredients. Finally, add the melted butter.

3 Beat the mixture lightly with a fork until all the flour is combined, but the mixture remains slightly lumpy. Fold in the fruit and rind, and spoon into the paper cases.

4 Bake for about 20 minutes or until a skewer inserted in the middle comes out cleanly. Serve warm or cold. Must be eaten on the same day as baking.

Cook's tip:

Don't be tempted to overbeat the mixture until smooth as this makes the muffins go flat.

Fruity Scones

Family Favourite

Old-fashioned fruit scones are delicious served split and buttered. These ones can be made and baked in under half an hour.

Ingredients:

225g/8oz self-raising flour
1 tsp baking powder
50g/2oz butter
25g/1oz golden caster sugar
75g/3oz mixed dried fruit
25g/1oz walnuts, chopped
1 egg
Just under 150ml/¼pt milk

15 minutes preparation
10-15 minutes baking
Makes 9 Scones

1 Preheat the oven to 220°C/425°F/Gas 7 and grease two baking sheets.

2 Sift the flour and baking powder into a bowl, add the butter and rub in until the mixture resembles fine crumbs. Stir in the sugar and fruit.

3 Break the egg into a measuring jug and bring the level up to 150ml/¼pt with milk. Beat and stir into the dry ingredients to make a soft dough. Place on a lightly floured surface and knead lightly until smooth.

4 Roll out the dough and cut into nine 5cm/2 inch rounds. Place on the baking sheets, brush the tops with milk and bake for 10 minutes or until golden. Cool and serve spilt in half and buttered.

Cook's tip:

- Dip the cutter into flour before cutting out the rounds.
- Scone dough should be soft and spongy. Handle very lightly for the best results.

Choc Rock Cakes

Quick and Easy

Making little rock cakes is an ideal way to introduce the kids to baking. This quick and easy mixture is lovely and messy for little fingers too!

Ingredients:

225g/8oz self-raising flour
A pinch of salt
75g/3oz butter or block margarine
1 tbsp caster sugar
1 egg, beaten
4-5 tbsp milk
100g/4oz chocolate chips
2 tbsp demerara sugar

15 minutes preparation
12 minutes baking
Makes 14 small cakes

1 Preheat the oven to 200°C/400°F/Gas 6. Lightly grease two baking sheets.

2 Sift the flour and salt into a bowl and add the butter cut into pieces. Rub in the fat until the mixture resembles fine crumbs. Stir in the sugar.

3 Add the egg and enough milk to make a soft mixture. Lightly knead in the chocolate chips.

4 Shape into 12-14 small heaps and place on the baking sheets. Bake for 12-15 minutes until firm and golden brown. Cool and sprinkle with sugar.

Cook's tip:

- Rock cakes are best eaten on the day of baking.
- For a variation, add 100g/4oz mixed dried fruit or chopped walnuts instead of chocolate chips.

Palmiers

The secret to making these heart-shaped pastries is in the folding of the pastry. Follow the instructions to make these light-as-air delicacies.

Ingredients:

450g/1lb packet puff pastry, thawed if frozen
175g/6oz demerara sugar

Filling:

140ml/¼pt double cream
1 tsp caster sugar
A few drops vanilla essence
225g/8oz fresh strawberries, halved

45 minutes preparation
20 minutes baking
Makes 12

1 Preheat the oven to 200°C/400°F/Gas 6. Cut the puff pastry in half. Scatter a working surface with 50g/2oz demerara sugar and roll half the pastry into a rectangle 30x25cm/12x10 inches. Trim to form straight edges and corners.

2 Fold the two long pastry edges over to meet in the centre. Lightly sprinkle the top with another 25g/1oz sugar, then take one side of the pastry and fold it over to cover the over half.

3 With a sharp knife, cut the folded pastry strip into 12 narrow slices 1.5cm/½ inch wide. Repeat the whole rolling and folding process with the other half of the pastry, then chill until needed.

4 Dampen a baking sheet and place six palmiers on the sheet, allowing room for them to spread. Pinch the joined end of each pastry together, then flatten out with the heel of your hands.

5 Bake the pastries towards the top of the oven for 15-20 minutes until light golden brown and the sugar on the outside has turned to caramel. Bake the remaining pastries in the same way.

6 For the filling, whip the cream until stiff, then fold in the vanilla essence and sugar. Place in a piping bag fitted with a star nozzle and pipe a heart on each pastry. Sandwich a plain pastry on top, pipe on a swirl of cream and decorate with a strawberry half.

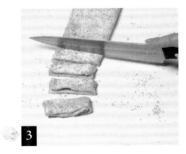

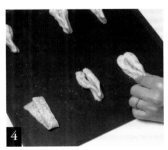

Macaroons

No Fat

Light as air, macaroons have a delicious, soft almond filling. Serve them with coffee or to accompany desserts.

Ingredients:

Rice paper sheets
100g/4oz ground almonds
175g/6oz caster sugar
2 egg whites
A few drops of almond
    essence

Decoration:

16 almond halves
Egg white to glaze
Caster sugar to sprinkle

15 minutes preparation
15 minutes baking
Makes 16

1 Preheat the oven to 180°C/350°F/Gas 4. Line two baking trays with rice paper sheets.

2 Stir the almonds and sugar together. Whisk the egg whites with the almond essence until stiff.

3 Gradually beat in the almonds and sugar until the mixture is a stiff paste. Spoon into a large piping bag fitted with a plain nozzle.

4 Pipe 16 small rounds on to the rice paper, spacing

them well apart. For the decoration, whisk the egg white lightly and brush over each round. Sprinkle lightly with caster sugar.

5 Press a halved almond into the centre of each round and bake for about 15 minutes or until the macaroons are just beginning to become pale golden. Cool on the trays until firm, then break away the rice paper to separate the cakes.

Cook's tip:

Store the macaroons in an airtight tin to keep them crisp and dry for up to 1 week. Don't use a plastic food storage box as this will encourage them to become moist and soft.

Mini Meringues

Easy Entertaining

For a special afternoon tea, make these delicious, crisp delicacies.

Ingredients:

75g/3oz caster sugar
75g/3oz golden caster sugar
3 egg whites
A pinch of cream of tartar

Filling:

100g/4oz plain chocolate
150m/¼pt double cream

30 minutes preparation
1½ hours baking
Makes 15 double meringues

1 Preheat the oven to 110°C/225°F/Gas ? Line two baking sheets with non-stick baking paper. Stir the sugars together.

2 Place the egg whites in a clean, dry, grease-free bowl and whisk with the cream of tartar until they are stiff.

3 Whisk in the sugar, a little at a time, making sure the meringue is stiff before the next addition.

4 Place the meringue in a piping bag fitted with a star nozzle. Pipe 30 small rounds on the paper. Bake for about 1½ hours, or until crisp and dry. Reverse the trays half way through the baking.

5 Leave to cool on a wire rack on the paper and slide away the paper when cold.

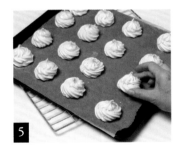

6 To make the filling, melt the chocolate in a bowl over a pan of warm water, or in the microwave on Low. Dip the underside of each meringue in the chocolate and leave to dry on non-stick paper. Whip the cream and sandwich the meringues together in pairs. Place in paper cases to serve.

Cook's tip:

Make the meringue bases ahead of time and store them, undecorated, in an airtight tin. Store for up to 3 days then dip in the chocolate and sandwich with cream just before serving.

Banana Fudge Muffins

Family Favourite

These moist, banana cup cakes contain mini pieces of fudge, with a toffee-flavoured icing. They don't last long in our household!

Ingredients:

175g/6oz ripe bananas
100g/4oz soft margarine
75g/3oz soft light brown sugar
50g/2oz soft caramel fudge
2 eggs
1 tbsp milk
225g/8oz plain flour
1 tsp baking powder

Topping:

100g/4oz golden, unrefined icing sugar
½ tsp butterscotch essence
10 dried banana chips

15 minutes preparation
20 minutes baking
Makes 10 large cakes

1 Preheat the oven to 180°C/350°F/Gas 4. Place 10 large paper muffin cases in deep muffin tins. Peel the bananas and mash the fruit in a bowl. Chop the fudge into small cubes.

2 Add the margarine, sugar, eggs and milk to the bowl with the bananas, then sift in the flour and baking powder. Beat together for 2 minutes until smooth. Stir in the fudge.

3 Divide between the paper cases. Bake the muffins for 20-25 minutes until a skewer inserted comes out cleanly. Cool on a wire rack.

4 For the topping, blend the icing sugar with the essence and 4 teaspoons of cold water and mix to a thin glacé icing. Spoon over the top of each cake, then top each one with a banana chip.

Cook's tip:

If you don't have deep muffin tins, bake the mixture in 24 small paper cases in bun trays for 15 minutes.

Pink Piggies

Party Special

Little cakes with an animal theme are always popular for children's parties. Why not get the kids to help you decorate them?

Ingredients:

100g/4oz soft-tub margarine
100g/4oz caster sugar
2 eggs
100g/4oz self-raising flour
A few drops of vanilla essence

Decoration:

Pink food colouring
100g/4oz fondant icing mix, or icing sugar
32 edible silver balls
Pink and yellow mini marshmallows

40 minutes preparation
20 minutes baking
Makes 16 small cakes

1 Preheat the oven to 180°C/350°F/ Gas 4. Line two bun trays with paper cases.

2 Place the margarine, eggs, sugar, flour and essence in a bowl and beat together for about 2 minutes until smooth. Half fill each paper case with the mixture.

3 Bake for about 20 minutes, then cool the buns on a wire rack. Cut the tops of the cakes level if they have peaked.

4 For the decoration, mix the icing sugar with a little water to make a thin icing. Add a little food colouring into the icing to make an even colour. Spoon a little on to each cake and spread out with a teaspoon.

5 Cut a marshmallow in half and position as ears. Place a marshmallow in the centre to form the snout. Position the silver balls as eyes and cut a yellow marshmallow in half for the mouth.

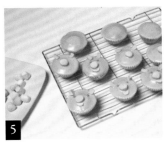

Blackberry Oysters

Freezer Friendly

I make a batch of these little pastries and freeze them. They are handy if you want to serve just a few for tea time with a selection of sandwiches.

Ingredients:

175g/6oz shortcrust pastry
60g/2¹/2oz butter or block
   margarine
60g/2¹/2oz caster sugar
25g/1oz self-raising flour
50g/2oz ground almonds
1 egg, beaten
A few drops of almond
   essence

Filling:

5 tablespoons blackberry
   jam
50g/2oz unsalted butter
100g/4oz icing sugar

30 minutes preparation
20 minutes baking
Makes 16

1 Preheat the oven to 190°C/375°F/Gas 5. Grease two patty tins. Roll out the pastry thinly, then cut out sixteen 7.5cm/3 inch rounds and press into the tins to line.

2 Beat the fat and sugar together until fluffy, then beat in the flour, almonds, egg and essence. Place a heaped teaspoonful in each pastry case and bake for about 20 minutes, until risen and golden. Cool on a wire rack.

3 When cold, scoop around the sponge filling with a knife and place a teaspoon of jam in the base of each pastry case.

4 For the filling, beat the butter with the icing sugar until light and fluffy. Pipe or spoon a little buttercream on top of the jam, then replace the sponge filling and dust with icing sugar to serve.

Cook's tip:

To freeze, complete the cakes, but do not dust with icing sugar. Freeze in a rigid plastic box to protect these delicate pastries. They keep for 2 months. Dust with icing sugar before serving.

baked *in a* tray

Flapjacks

Quick and Easy

Everybody loves these sweet, sticky, oaty squares. I like to make mine with honey and add dried cranberries for their hint of sharpness – but try your own versions. Add dried fruits or apricots, cherries, nuts or apple slices – the variations are endless.

Ingredients:

100g/4oz butter or margarine
75g/3oz golden syrup or honey
75g/3oz soft light brown sugar
200g/7oz porridge oats
25g/1oz wholewheat flour
50g/2oz dried cranberries or sultanas

10 minutes preparation
25 minutes baking
Makes 12

1 Preheat the oven to 180°C/350°F/Gas 4. Grease and line the base of a 20cm/8 inch shallow, square tin.

2 Put the butter, syrup or honey and sugar in a saucepan and heat gently until dissolved.

3 Add the oats, flour and cranberries or sultanas and stir well. Spoon into the tin and spread level.

4 Bake for about 25 minutes, until golden. Mark into 12 fingers while still warm, then leave to cool in the tin. Peel the papers away and store in an airtight tin until needed.

Cook's tip:

To freeze, wrap the cold flapjack tightly in foil. Keep frozen for up to 2 months.

Spicy Fudge Traybake

spicy

If you are asked to bake for the school fair or charity events, this frosted tray bake is an easy one to make from store cupboard ingredients.

Ingredients:

100g/4oz soft-tub margarine
100g/4oz golden caster sugar
75g/3oz wholewheat flour
50g/2oz self-raising flour
1 tsp baking powder
1/2 tsp ground cinnamon
2 eggs
2 tbsp milk
1 tbsp golden syrup

Icing:

175g/6oz golden icing sugar
50g/2oz softened butter
1 tbsp milk

20 minutes preparation
20 minutes baking
Makes 16 slices

1 Preheat the oven to 180°C/350°F/Gas 4. Grease and line an 18x27cm/7x11 inch shallow tin with non-stick baking paper.

2 Place the margarine and sugar in a bowl and sift in the flours, baking powder and spice. Add the eggs, milk and syrup and beat for 2 minutes until smooth.

3 Spoon into the tin and smooth the top level. Bake for 20-25 minutes until the cake is springy and has shrunk away from the sides of the tin. Loosen around the sides of the tin with a palette knife, then turn out to cool completely on a wire rack.

4 For the icing, place the icing ingredients in a bowl and beat until smooth. Swirl the frosting over the top of the cake with a palette knife.

5 Place the cake on a board and cut the cake into 16 oblong slices with a sharp knife.

Espresso Squares

Freezer Friendly

If you like coffee, you'll love these moist little squares with a coffee-cream lattice. I often make a batch of these, serving half and storing the other half in the freezer.

30 minutes preparation
25 minutes baking
Makes 15 squares

Ingredients:

175g/6oz self-raising flour
1 tsp baking powder
175g/6 oz soft-tub margarine
175g/6oz soft light brown sugar
3 eggs
2 tbsp coffee essence

Icing:

75g/3oz softened butter
175g/6oz golden icing sugar, sifted
1 tbsp coffee essence

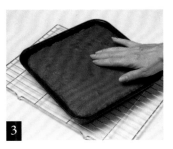

1 Preheat the oven to 180°C/350°F/Gas 4. Grease and line the base of a 23cm/9 inch square cake tin with non-stick baking paper.

2 Sift the flour and baking powder into a bowl and add the remaining cake ingredients. Beat together with a wooden spoon for about 2 minutes until smooth.

3 Spoon into the tin and smooth the surface level. Bake for 25-30 minutes until well-risen and firm. Test by pressing the centre lightly with

the fingertips. Cool in the tin for 5 minutes then turn out on to a wire rack and peel away the lining paper.

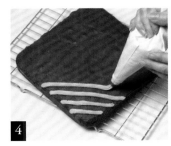

4 To make the icing, place the butter, sugar and essence in a bowl and whisk until smooth. Spoon the icing into a piping bag fitted with a star nozzle. Pipe a criss-cross lattice pattern over the top of the cake.

5 Place the cake on a board and cut into 15 squares, using a sharp knife.

Cook's tip:

If you don't have a piping bag, simply spread the icing over with a palette knife, then make a wiggly pattern with a fork.

Millionaire's Shortbread

Something special

You'll always be popular with your guests when you serve these chocolate-topped, luxury layers.

Ingredients:

100g/4oz butter, softened
50g/2oz golden caster sugar
175g/6oz plain flour

Topping:

175g/6oz plain chocolate,
broken into squares

Caramel:

400g/14oz can condensed
milk
2 tbsp golden syrup
100g/4oz golden caster
sugar
100g/4oz butter

1 hour 30 minutes preparation
25 minutes baking
Makes 9 squares

3

1 Preheat the oven to 180°C/350°F/Gas 4. Grease and line the base of a 20cm/8 inch square tin with non-stick baking paper.

2 Beat the butter and sugar together until pale and fluffy. Mix in the flour and knead in the bowl until smooth.

3 Press the mixture into the tin and prick the surface with a fork. Bake for 20-25 minutes until light golden. Cool in the tin on a wire rack.

4 To make the caramel layer, put the condensed milk, syrup, sugar and butter in a heavy-based saucepan. Heat gently until every grain of sugar has dissolved.

5 Bring to the boil and boil for 6-8 minutes, stirring continuously, until light golden and thickened. Pour the caramel over the biscuit base to cover it completely. Leave until cold and set.

6 Melt the chocolate in a bowl standing over a pan of warm water, or alternatively, in the microwave on Low. Spread over the caramel with a palette knife and leave to cool and set. Mark into 9 squares to serve.

5

6

Bread & Butter Pudding

Family Favourite

Family desserts need not be expensive affairs. This favourite recipe uses up ordinary sliced white bread, making it into a creamy, light-as-air pudding.

45 minutes preparation
40 minutes baking
Serves 6

Ingredients:

12 thin slices of white bread
75g/3oz butter, softened
100g/4oz sultanas
Finely grated rind of 2 lemons
100g/4oz demerara sugar
300ml/¹/₂pt milk
150ml/¹/₄pt single cream
3 eggs
Few drops of vanilla essence

1 Cut the crusts from the bread and spread one side of each slice with butter. Cut each slice in half diagonally, then in half again to make four triangles.

2 Butter a 1.7l/3pt ovenproof tin or dish and arrange the triangles in an overlapping pattern, scattering the sultanas, lemon rind and sugar in-between the layers.

3 Beat the milk, cream, eggs and essence together, pour over the bread and leave to soak for 30 minutes.

4 Preheat the oven to 180°C/350°F/Gas 4. Bake the pudding for about 40 minutes until the slices are crisp and golden and the custard mixture has set.

5 Serve cut into squares, sprinkled with extra sugar, with thick cream or dairy custard.

Cook's tip:

For a variation, spread 3 tablespoons of orange marmalade on to the bread with the butter, and scatter over dried, no-soak apricots instead of sultanas.

Autumn Crumble Bake

Family Favourite

Young or old, all the family love a fruit-based crumble. It must be the easiest dessert to make. If you make the crumble topping in the food processor, you won't even get your hands dirty.

Ingredients:

450g/1lb cooking apples, peeled, cored and chopped
450g/1lb ripe plums, stoned, quartered
3 tbsp golden granulated sugar

Topping:

175g/6oz plain flour
75g/3oz butter or block margarine, diced
50g/2oz golden caster sugar

15 minutes preparation
40 minutes baking
Serves 6

1 Preheat the oven to 200°C/400°F/Gas 6. Put the apples in a heavy-based pan, add 125ml/4fl oz water and bring to the boil. Cover and simmer for 5 minutes.

2 Drain the apples and add the plums and sugar. Mix and place in an oblong shallow 1.7l/3pt dish or a 23cm/9 inch square, shallow baking tray.

3 To make the crumble topping, sift the flour into a bowl and add the fat. Rub into the mixture with your fingertips until the mixture resembles fine crumbs, then stir in the sugar.

4 Spoon the mixture over the fruit in the dish and spread level. Bake for 35-40 minutes, or until the crumble topping is golden and the fruit is tender.

Cook's tip:

If plums are not in season, use 450g/1lb firm dessert pears. For a summer version, use 250g/9oz strawberries and 4 firm sliced peaches mixed with 4 tablespoons of granulated sugar.

Lemon Meringue Squares

Easy Entertaining

This tray bake is a cross between a lemon meringue pie and a cake, so you can serve it either as a pudding or for afternoon tea.

Cake Layer:

75g/3oz butter
75g/3oz caster sugar
2 eggs
100g/4oz self-raising flour

Meringue:

2 egg whites
100g/4oz caster sugar

Lemon Filling:

50g/2oz butter
50g/2oz caster sugar
2 egg yolks
Finely grated rind of 1 lemon
2 tbsp lemon juice

50 minutes preparation
1 hour baking
Makes 12

1 Preheat the oven to 160°C/325°F/Gas 3. Grease and line the base of an 18x27cm/7x11 inch baking tray with non-stick baking paper.

2 Place the lemon filling ingredients in a heatproof bowl over a pan of hot water and stir until the butter dissolves. The mixture should be thick enough to coat the back of a wooden spoon. Cool the mixture.

3 Make the cake layer. Beat the butter with the sugar until light and fluffy then beat in the eggs one at a time, adding a little flour with each. Fold in the remaining flour and spread into the tin.

4 Spread the cooled lemon filling over the top of the sponge mixture. Make the meringue topping. Whisk the egg whites until stiff, then fold in half the sugar and whisk again until stiff. Fold in the remaining sugar.

5 Spoon the meringue over the top of the filling, covering it completely. Bake for 1 hour until the top is crisp and light golden. Using a very sharp knife, cut into 12 squares.

Apple Pie for a Crowd

Easy Entertaining

I love making the most of the local varieties of apples available every autumn, and really enjoy a trip to our local farmer's market to buy trays of glorious fruits to bake into pies.

Pastry:

100g/4oz self-raising flour
225g/8oz plain flour
A pinch of salt
1 tbsp caster sugar
175g/6oz butter or block
**   margarine**

Filling:

900g/2lb cooking apples,
Juice and finely grated rind
**   of ½ lemon**
2 tsp plain flour
½ tsp ground cinnamon
½ tsp ground nutmeg
100g/4oz golden caster sugar
15g/½oz butter
1 egg white, beaten
Caster sugar to glaze

35 minutes preparation
45 minutes baking
Serves 6-8

1 To make the pastry, sift the flours, salt and sugar into a bowl. Add the butter, cutting it into small cubes. Rub the fat into the flour with your fingertips until it resembles fine crumbs. Add 5-6 tablespoons of cold water and mix together with a knife. Knead to a soft dough then wrap in clingfilm and chill for 1 hour.

2 Preheat the oven to 200°C/400°F/Gas 6. Mix the flour, spices and sugar together. Peel, core and chop the apples, then toss in the lemon juice and rind, and the sugar mixture. Place in the base of a 1.7l/3pt oblong tray or dish, or a 23cm/9 inch round pie dish and dot with butter.

3 Roll two-thirds of the pastry out to an oblong 2.5cm/1 inch larger than the top of the dish. Moisten the edges of the dish with water. Roll thin strips to make a border around the pie dish and press into the sides.

4 Place the pastry lid on top, cutting a hole in the centre. Roll out the trimmings and make into fancy shapes to decorate. Brush with beaten egg white and sprinkle lightly with sugar. Bake for 40-45 minutes until crisp and golden.

Cherry Cheesecake Slices

These cherry cheesecake slices make the ideal dessert for a picnic, or make a tray of them ahead of time and serve them after a barbecue.

Ingredients:

175g/6oz digestive biscuits
75g/3oz butter, melted
25g/1oz golden granulated sugar

Topping:

400g/14oz jar pitted morello cherries
2 tsp arrowroot

Filling:

350g/12oz full-fat cream cheese
100g/4oz natural caster sugar
2 eggs, beaten
1/2 tsp vanilla essence
2 tsp lemon juice

45 minutes preparation
30 minutes baking
Makes 12 slices

1 Preheat the oven to 180°C/350°F/Gas 4. Grease and line the base of an 18x27cm/7x11 inch oblong tin with non-stick baking paper. Place the biscuits in a strong plastic food bag and crush into crumbs by tapping with a rolling pin.

2 Melt the butter in a heavy-based pan and mix in the biscuit crumbs and sugar. Stir together, then spoon into the tin and spread over the base evenly.

3 Soften the cream cheese together with the sugar, then beat in the eggs, essence and lemon juice until smooth. Pour over the biscuit base in

the tin. Bake for about 30 minutes until the filling is risen, firm and golden. Cool in the tin, then chill. When cold, remove from the tin and peel away the papers.

4 To make the cherry topping, dissolve the arrowroot powder with 2 tablespoons of juice from the cherries. Place the cherries and remaining juice in a heavy-based pan and heat until the juices thicken. Spoon the cherry mixture over the baked base.

5 Leave to cool and set, then cut into 12 slices with a sharp knife.

Luxury Bread Pudding

Freezer Friendly

This easy recipe will get you out of a fix when you have promised to contribute to the kid's bring-&-buy sale – and then forgotten to buy any ingredients! Use up all the left-over bread in the house, and add a few store cupboard ingredients.

Ingredients:

450g/1lb stale bread, crusts removed
Finely grated rind and juice of 1 orange
300ml/¹/₂pt milk
1 egg
225g/8oz dried mixed fruit
100g/4oz soft dark brown sugar
75g/3oz soft-tub margarine
1 tsp mixed spice
3 tbsp fine cut marmalade, warmed
1 tbsp ginger wine or orange liqueur (optional)
2 tbsp golden granulated sugar

30 minutes preparation
1 hour baking
Makes 16 slices

1 Preheat the oven to 190°C/375°F/Gas 5. Grease an 18x28cm/7x11 inch oblong tin.

2 Cut the bread into small pieces. Place in a large bowl with the orange rind, juice and milk. Leave to soak for 15 minutes. Mash with a fork to break up the pieces.

3 Add the egg, dried fruit, brown sugar, margarine, spice, marmalade and liqueur and stir together.

4 Spread into the tin and smooth the surface level. Bake for about 1 hour, or until firm. Cool in the tin and dredge the top with granulated sugar.

5 Cut into 16 slices then serve warm or cold.

Cook's tip:
To freeze, wrap in foil. Freeze for up to 6 months.

cookies

Melting Moments

Quick and Easy

These little biscuits couldn't be easier. Just roll the mixture into a ball and pop in a piece of cherry. They really do melt in the mouth!

Ingredients:

40g/1½oz caster sugar
50g/2oz butter or block margarine
A few drops of vanilla essence
75g/3oz self-raising flour
15g/½oz rolled oats or desiccated coconut
4 glacé cherries

10 minutes preparation
15 minutes baking
Makes 16

1 Preheat the oven to 180°C/350°F/Gas 4. Grease two baking sheets.

2 Beat the caster sugar, butter or margarine and vanilla essence together until fluffy.

3 Sift in the flour and mix with your fingertips to make a soft dough. Divide into 16 pieces.

4 Roll each piece into a ball. Spread the oats or coconut out on to a plate and roll each ball to coat it. Flatten each ball slightly.

5 Cut each cherry into four and place one piece on every biscuit. Place on the prepared baking sheets and bake for about 15 minutes until the biscuits are puffed up and pale golden.

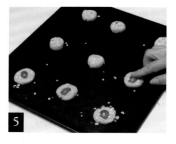

Cook's tip:

Store the baked cookies in an airtight tin and they will keep crisp for up to 3 days. Do not store in a plastic food container, as these are designed to keep in moisture and will make the biscuits go soft.

Coconut & Lemon Cookies

Freezer Friendly

Although these cookies may look plain, the combination of sharp lemon and sweet crunchy coconut is extremely tasty.

Ingredients:

100g/4oz butter or margarine
150g/5oz soft light brown sugar
100g/4oz plain flour
50g/2oz self-raising flour
75g/3oz porridge oats
50g/2oz desiccated coconut
1 lemon
1 tsp vanilla essence
1 egg

10 minutes preparation
12 minutes baking
Makes 24

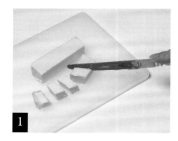

1 Preheat the oven to 180°C/350°F/Gas 4. Grease two baking sheets. Chop the butter or margarine into small cubes.

2 Stir the sugar, flours, oats and coconut together in a bowl. Finely grate the zest from the lemon and add to the bowl.

3 Beat the egg and vanilla together and add to the bowl with 1 tablespoon of lemon juice. Mix to a soft mixture.

4 Place 24 heaped teaspoons of mixture on to the baking sheets and flatten out slightly. Bake for 12 minutes until light golden and firm. Remove from the sheets with a palette knife and cool on wire racks.

Cook's tip:

Space the biscuits evenly on the baking sheets, leaving room for them to spread. Flatten them with wetted fingers into neat shapes.

Crunchy Peanut Butter Cookies

Quick and Easy

Who can resist these crunchy morsels? You can make these cookies from store cupboard ingredients – a great way to keep the kids busy on a rainy day.

Ingredients:

50g/2oz soft-tub margarine
100g/4oz crunchy peanut butter
75g/3oz caster sugar
100g/4oz self-raising flour
1/2 tsp bicarbonate of soda
1 egg, beaten
50g/2oz porridge oats
50g/2oz shelled peanuts, chopped
1-2 tbsp milk

10 minutes preparation
10-12 minutes baking
Makes 16

1 Preheat the oven to 190°C/375°F/Gas 5. Grease two baking sheets.

2 Beat the margarine, peanut butter and sugar together until light and fluffy.

3 Sift in the flour and bicarbonate of soda and stir together with the egg, oats, peanuts and enough milk to form a soft dough.

4 Roll heaped tablespoons of the mixture into balls. Space them well apart on the baking sheets, slightly flatten, then press down with a fork.

5 Bake for 15 minutes until golden. Cool on the baking sheets for 2 minutes to firm up, then with a palette knife lift on to a wire rack to cool.

Cook's tip:

If you lightly wet your hands when you roll the dough into balls, you will find the mixture does not stick.

Giant Choc Chip Cookies

Family Favourite

You'll find these giant cookies on sale in fancy bakers – delicious, but they can be pricey! Make this version for a lot fewer pennies.

15 minutes preparation
15 minutes baking
Makes 12-14

Ingredients:

175g/6oz self-raising flour
25g/1oz cocoa powder
75g/3oz soft-tub slightly salted butter or margarine
50g/2oz granulated sugar
50g/2oz golden caster sugar
1 egg, beaten
1 tsp vanilla essence
50g/2oz plain chocolate chips
25g/1oz white chocolate chips
2 tsp milk

1 Preheat the oven to 180°C/350°F/Gas 4. Lightly grease two baking sheets. Sift the flour and cocoa into a bowl.

2 Place all the ingredients (except the chocolate chips) in a bowl and mix thoroughly to make a soft, smooth dough. Gradually work in the chocolate chips.

3 Place 6 large spoonfuls of the mixture, well apart, on each baking sheet and flatten slightly with the back of a wetted spoon.

4 Bake for 15-20 minutes until risen, light golden and just firm to the touch. Leave on the trays to firm for 2-3 minutes, then lift on to a wire rack to cool using a palette knife.

Cook's tip:

Don't be tempted to overcrowd the trays as the cookies will spread out during cooking. If you don't have enough baking sheets, divide the mixture in half and reuse the same baking sheet, cooling it and re-greasing it each time.

Gingerbread Bears

Party Special

These cute little critters appeal to children of all ages. Make them for a children's party and just watch the adults sneak them off the plates!

Ingredients:

225g/8oz plain flour
1 tsp bicarbonate of soda
½ tsp ground ginger
½ tsp mixed spice
50g/2oz butter or block margarine
50g/2oz golden syrup
50g/2oz soft dark brown sugar
½ egg, beaten

To decorate:

50g/2oz royal icing sugar

30 minutes preparation
10 minutes baking
Makes 20 large or 28 small cookies

1 Preheat the oven to 170°C/350°F/Gas 3 and grease two baking sheets. Sift the flour into a bowl with the bicarbonate of soda and the spices. Melt the butter in a saucepan with the syrup and sugar.

2 Pour the melted mixture into the dry ingredients, add the egg and mix to a soft dough. Knead gently. The dough will be sticky at first, but it will firm as it cools.

3 Roll out to about 3cm/⅛ inch thickness and cut out fancy shapes. Bake for about 10-12 minutes and leave to firm for 2 minutes. Then remove to cooling racks with a palette knife.

4 To decorate, mix the royal icing sugar with water to make a piping consistency. Place in a small piping bag and pipe on buttons, bow ties, frills or fancy decorations.

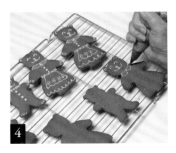

Cook's tip:
Keep checking the cookies towards the end of the baking time, as they can over-brown very quickly.

Cantucci Biscotti

No Fat

These delicious almond biscuits are baked until they are very dry. They are meant to be served dipped into a sweet Italian wine called Vin Santo, but are equally delicious with creamy desserts or coffee.

Ingredients:

250g/9oz plain flour
2 tsp baking powder
A pinch of salt
175g/6oz caster sugar
2 eggs
1 tsp vanilla essence
1 tbsp amaretto liqueur
150g/5oz blanched whole almonds

45 minutes preparation
35 minutes baking
Makes 24

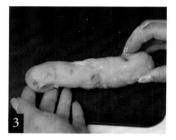

1 Preheat the oven to 180°C/350°F/Gas 4. Grease and flour two baking sheets.

2 Sift the flour, baking powder and salt into a bowl and stir in the sugar. Beat the eggs with the essence and liqueur. Add to the bowl with the almonds and mix to a very soft dough.

3 Divide into 4 equal pieces and roll each into a log shape about 15cm/6 inches long. Chill in the freezer for 5 minutes to firm the dough.

Place on the baking sheets and bake for 20 minutes until golden.

4 Remove from the oven and cut each log into 1cm/½ inch slices while still warm. Separate them and lay on a baking sheet.

5 Return the biscuits to the oven and bake for 15 minutes until golden, turning them over half way through the cooking. Cool completely then store in an airtight tin.

Cook's tip:

Place two pieces of dough only on each baking sheet, as the dough will spread out during baking.

Butterscotch Nut Thins

Easy Entertaining

These luxurious, wafer-thin biscuits are delicious served with vanilla ice cream, or on their own with a cup of coffee. They could not be easier to make. Just melt the mixture together in a saucepan.

Ingredients:

Sheets of rice paper
40g/1½oz butter
40g/1½oz caster sugar
2 tsp double cream or rich milk
75g/3oz chopped or flaked almonds

10 minutes preparation
8 minutes baking
Makes 14-16

1 Preheat the oven to 180°C/350°F/Gas 4. Line two baking baking trays with sheets of rice paper, overlapping them if necessary.

2 Place the butter, sugar and cream in a heavy-based pan and heat gently until melted. Bring to the boil, then simmer for 30 seconds until light and foaming. Remove from the heat, stir in the nuts and mix thoroughly.

3 Place 8 heaped teaspoonfuls on the rice paper on each tray. Space well apart as the biscuits will spread out during cooking.

4 Bake for 8 minutes until a medium golden colour. Leave on the trays until firm, then lift up and break off the extra rice paper. Store in an airtight tin.

Cook's tip:

These biscuits will turn brown and caramelise very quickly, so be careful to watch them towards the end of cooking.

Fruity Florentines

Easy Entertaining

You'll find these luxury biscuits on sale in expensive delis and food departments. Make your own colourful version, full of good things, as an ideal gift for a hostess, or even a super Christmas present.

Ingredients:

75g/3oz butter
100g/4oz icing sugar, sifted
4 tbsp double cream
15g/¹/₂oz glacé cherries,
    chopped
15g/¹/₂oz angelica, chopped
15g/¹/₂oz crystalised ginger,
    chopped
40g/1¹/₂oz plain flour

2 tsp lemon juice
75g/3oz mixed peel
25g/1oz currants
75g/3oz flaked almonds

Topping:

75g/3oz plain chocolate,
    melted

25 minutes preparation
10-12 minutes baking
Makes 15-20

1 Preheat the oven to 190°C/375°F/Gas 5. Line two baking sheets with non-stick baking paper. Gently heat the butter, icing sugar and cream in a saucepan.

2 When the butter has melted, add the rest of the ingredients and mix together in the pan using a wooden spoon.

3 Spoon dessertspoonfuls of the mixture on to the

sheets, leaving a 7.5cm/3 inch space between each one to allow the mixture to spread. Bake for 10-12 minutes until the edges are golden and lacy. Cool the trays for 10 minutes, then transfer to a cooling rack.

4 When cold, brush the backs of the biscuits with melted chocolate and leave to set for 30 minutes.

Cook's tip:

If the biscuits spread unevenly, pat them into a round shape with a knife or pastry cutter, while still hot on the trays.

Shortbread

Easy Entertaining

I make this crumbly, buttery favourite every December for New Year's Eve. We always observe the Scots tradition of first footing – taking some shortbread and a piece of coal to our friends and neighbours.

30 minutes preparation
25 minutes baking
Makes 8 wedges

Ingredients:

100g/4oz butter
50g/2oz caster sugar
Finely grated zest of ½ lemon
150g/5oz plain flour
25g/1oz ground rice or cornflour
Caster sugar for dusting

1 Preheat the oven to 170°C/325°F/Gas 3. Grease a baking sheet. Beat the butter and sugar together with the lemon zest until pale and fluffy.

2 Sift the flour and ground rice or cornflour into the mixture and bring it together with your fingertips to make a soft dough. Roll out the dough on a floured surface to make an 18cm/7 inch circle.

3 Place on the baking sheet and crimp the edges with your fingers.

4 Mark into 8 wedges, then prick the dough all over with a fork. Chill in the freezer for 5 minutes.

5 Bake for 25-30 minutes until the shortbread is pale golden and firm to the touch. Cool on the baking sheet for 15 minutes, then transfer to a wire rack until cold. Cut into wedges and serve sprinkled with caster sugar.

Cook's tip:

Store the shortbread in an airtight tin for up to 1 week or freeze, wrapped in foil, for up to 2 months.

Mocha Pinwheels

Freezer Friendly

Keep this fancy biscuit dough stored in the freezer until you are ready to bake it, then you'll always have fresh cookies to offer.

Vanilla layer:

50g/2oz butter or block margarine, softened
25g/1oz caster sugar
75g/3oz plain flour
A few drops of vanilla essence

Mocha layer:

50g/2oz butter or block margarine, softened
25g/1oz caster sugar
75g/3oz plain flour
1 tbsp cocoa powder
1 tsp coffee essence

1 hour preparation
20 minutes baking
Makes 18

1 Place the ingredients for the two doughs into separate bowls. Bring the ingredients for the vanilla dough together and bind to a soft dough with a tablespoon of water. Wrap and freeze for 15 minutes.

2 Bring the mocha ingredients together and bind to a soft dough. Wrap and freeze for 15 minutes.

3 Roll out each dough to a rectangle 18x25cm/7x10 inches. Brush the mocha dough with a little water, then place the vanilla dough on top.

4 Roll both doughs together like a Swiss roll from the narrow end. Wrap the dough and chill for 30 minutes, or freeze until firm.

5 Preheat the oven to 180°C/350°F/Gas 4. Grease two baking sheets. Cut the dough into 18 slices each 6cm/¼ inch wide.

6 Place on the baking sheets and space well apart. Bake for 15-20 minutes until firm and pale golden. Cool on the trays for 2 minutes to firm, then transfer on to a wire rack.

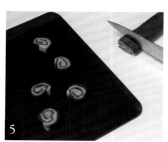

something special

Pina Colada Gateau

Party Special

This cake makes an ideal centrepiece for a summer party in the garden, or a special birthday cake. Make it ahead of time and store in the fridge for up to 1 day.

Ingredients:

175g/6oz soft margarine
175g/6oz caster sugar
3 eggs, beaten
175g/6oz self-raising flour
50g/2oz desiccated coconut

Filling and Decoration:

4250ml/³/₄pt double cream
1 tbsp Malibu or coconut liqueur
4 slices canned pineapple rings
50g/2oz coconut curls

45 minutes preparation
25 minutes baking
Serves 10

1 Preheat the oven to 180°C/350°F/Gas 4. Grease and line two 20cm/8 inch round, sandwich cake tins.

2 Make the cake bases. Place all the cake ingredients in a large bowl and beat together for about 2 minutes until smooth.

3 If the mixture is too dry, add 2 tablespoons of milk to form a soft consistency that drops from a spoon. Spoon into the tins and smooth level.

4 Bake for 25 minutes until the cakes are firm and shrink away from the tins. Stand for 5 minutes, then cool on a wire rack. Spread the coconut curls on to a baking

sheet and toast lightly for 1-2 minutes.

5 To make the filling, whip the cream until it forms soft peaks, then fold in the liqueur. Chop 3 of the pineapple rings and fold into half the cream and use to sandwich the cakes together.

6 Cut the remaining pineapple ring into 8 wedges. Spread cream around the sides of the cake and roll in the coconut curls. Spread cream over the top of the cake. Put the remaining cream in a piping bag with a star nozzle. Pipe 8 rosettes or stars around the edge and decorate each with a pineapple wedge.

Apricot Meringue Mountain

Easy Entertaining

This is one of my favourite desserts – light-as-a-feather meringue, sandwiched together with luscious cream and fruit. Try it with a fresh strawberry filling instead of apricot.

Ingredients:

225g/8oz caster sugar
4 large egg whites
¼ tsp cream of tartar

Filling:

300g/½pt double cream
400g/14oz can apricots in syrup

20 minutes preparation

50 minutes baking

Serves 6

1 Preheat the oven to 150°C/300°F/Gas 2. Draw a 23cm/9 inch circle on a sheet of non-stick baking paper, and a 15cm/6 inch circle on another and place the papers on two baking sheets.

2 Place the egg whites in a large, clean and dry bowl and whisk with the cream of tartar until stiff.

3 Gradually add the sugar a tablespoon at a time until the meringue is stiff and glossy.

4 Spoon the mixture on to the papers and spread out to fill the circles. Build or flick up the sides to form a rim. Turn the oven down to 140°C/275°F/Gas 1 and bake for 50 minutes or until the meringue is crisp. Cool completely on wire racks.

5 For the filling, whip the cream until stiff and spread in the large meringue case. Drain the apricots and place on top of the cream. Top with the small meringue and serve immediately.

Cook's tip:

• To make sure the bowl is completely grease-free, scald it out with boiling water and dry with kitchen paper. If there is any grease at all in the bowl, the egg whites will not whisk up.
• To test if the meringue is crisp and dry, push it slightly on the baking sheet. If it slides away from the paper easily, it is ready.

Christmas Log

Party Special

The Yule Log, served for Boxing Day tea, is a traditional part of Christmas time.

Ingredients:

2 tbsp cocoa
3 eggs
100g/4oz caster sugar
90g/3½ oz plain flour
2 tbsp caster sugar

Decoration:

1 tbsp cocoa powder
225g/8oz unsalted butter
450g/1lb golden icing sugar
3 tbsp milk
Icing sugar for dusting

45 minutes preparation
15 minutes baking
Serves 6

1 Preheat the oven to 200°C/400°F/Gas 6. Grease and line a 30x20cm/12x8 inch Swiss roll tin with non-stick baking paper.

2 Blend the cocoa powder with 3 tablespoons of boiling water and mix until smooth. Whisk the eggs and sugar in a heatproof bowl, set over a pan of hot water for 8 minutes until very pale and thick, or until the whisks leave a trail on the surface when lifted. Remove from the heat.

3 Sift in half the flour and fold in gently. Fold in the remaining flour with the cocoa mixture and stir until evenly blended. Pour the mixture into the tin and bake for 10-15 minutes until springy. Sprinkle the caster sugar over a sheet

of non-stick paper.

4 Turn the sponge on to the paper, peel away the lining paper and trim the sponge edges. Roll up from the long side with the paper inside and cool. When cold, carefully unroll the cake.

5 Make the icing. Blend the cocoa to a paste with 2 tablespoons of boiling water. Beat the icing sugar with the butter and milk until fluffy. Spread one-quarter of the buttercream over the Swiss roll and roll up. Add the cocoa mixture to the remaining buttercream and beat until smooth. Spread over the top and sides of the Swiss roll with a palette knife. Dust with icing sugar just before serving.

Cook's tip:

To make sure the cake rises evenly, tilt the Swiss roll tin so that the mixture covers the surface and fills the corners evenly.

Birthday Cake

Party Special

If you are asked to make a birthday cake in a hurry, this quick and easy one fits the bill. There is no difficult icing and you can vary the colours and decorations to suit all ages.

Ingredients:

175g/6oz soft-tub margarine
175g/6oz caster sugar
3 eggs, beaten
175g/6oz self-raising flour
1/2 tsp baking powder
1 tsp vanilla essence
2 tb sp milk
Pink food colouring

Icing and Filling:

100g/4oz apricot jam,
**   sieved, warmed**
275g/10oz ready-to-roll icing
Coloured birthday candles
**   and ribbons to decorate**

35 minutes preparation
25 minutes baking
Serves 8

1 Preheat the oven to 190°C/375°F/Gas 5. Grease two 19cm/7¹/2 inch sandwich tins and line the bases with non-stick baking paper. Put all the cake ingredients (except the colouring) in a bowl.

2 Beat for 2 minutes until pale and fluffy. Divide the mixture in two and colour one half pink. Spoon into the tins and spread the tops level. Bake for 20-25 minutes, or until just firm to the touch. Turn out to cool on a wire rack.

3 Spread one cake with a third of the jam, then top with the second cake. Spread the remaining jam over the top and sides.

4 Colour the icing pale pink then roll out on a surface dusted with icing sugar to a circle large enough to cover the top and sides of the cake. Lift on to the cake with both hands and smooth into position. Trim away the edges and press the candles into the top. Tie ribbons around the sides to serve.

Cook's tip:

Use paste food colouring to colour ready-to-roll icing as liquid food colouring will make the icing wet and unmanageable.

Rich Fruit Cake

Easy Entertaining

I always make this rich fruit cake 3-4 months ahead for Christmas or a special anniversary. This allows time for the flavours to mellow and the texture to become moist.

Ingredients:

900g/2lb mixed dried fruit
50g/2oz glacé cherries, washed, chopped
3 tbsp dark rum
Finely grated rind and juice of 1 lemon
225g/8oz soft dark muscovado sugar
225g/8oz butter, softened
2 tbsp black treacle
5 eggs, beaten
225g/8oz plain flour
1 tbsp mixed spice

1 hour preparation
3½ hours baking
Serves 10-12

1 Place the fruit in a large saucepan with 2 tablespoons of the rum and the lemon juice and rind, and heat to a simmer. Heat for 5 minutes, turning the fruit over in the liquid with a wooden spoon. Pour the fruit into a bowl, cover and leave to stand for 24 hours.

2 Preheat the oven to 150°C/300°F/Gas 2. Grease and double line the base and sides of a 20cm/8 inch round, deep cake tin. Beat the butter and sugar together until fluffy.

3 Beat in the eggs gradually, adding a teaspoon of flour with each addition. Beat in the treacle, then sift in the flour and spice.

4 Add the soaked fruit and stir well until the mixture is smooth. Spoon into the tin and smooth the top evenly.

5 Bake for 1 hour, then reduce the temperature to 140°C/275°F/Gas 1 and bake for a further 3-3½ hours or until a skewer inserted into the middle comes out cleanly.

6 Spoon the remaining tablespoon of rum over the warm cake and leave to cool in the tin. When cold, wrap in greaseproof paper, then tightly wrap in foil and store for 1-3 months.

Christmas Cake

Something Special

Follow these easy steps to decorate the ideal Christmas cake. Add a different ribbon to make an anniversary or christening cake.

Ingredients:

One 20cm/8 inch rich fruit cake (see page 241)
25cm/10 inch round cake board
4 tbsp sieved apricot jam
675g/1lb 8oz almond paste
1kg/2lb 2oz ready-to-roll icing
Golden balls
Wired ribbon

1 hour 30 minutes preparation
3 days drying
Serves 10-12

1 Place the cake on the cake board and brush all over with sieved apricot jam. Roll out one-third of the almond paste on a surface dusted with icing sugar. Using the cake tin as a guide, cut out a round, slightly larger than the top of the cake. Lift the disc of almond paste on to the cake with a rolling pin.

2 Use a length of string to measure the length and height of the sides of the cake. Roll the remaining almond paste to these measurements in a long strip. Roll up the strip, then loosely unroll around the cake and press the top and sides of the paste together. Leave the almond paste to dry out for 3 days in a cool place.

3 On a surface dusted with icing sugar roll out the ready-to-roll icing to make a circle large enough to cover the top and sides of the cake. Brush the almond paste with a little water to dampen it. Lift the icing over the cake to position it, then smooth down over the top and sides and press on to the cake. Trim away the edges.

4 While the icing is soft, mark lines across the top with the edge of a palette knife or a plastic rule. Mark another set in the opposite direction to make a square, cushioned effect. Place a golden ball in each square. Trim the cake with a festive ribbon to finish.

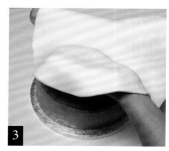

Gingerbread House

Party Special

This is a great way to keep the kids occupied in the days before Christmas.

Ingredients:

75g/3oz soft dark
   muscovado sugar
100g/4oz golden syrup
100g/4oz black treacle
75g/3oz block margarine
450g/1lb plain flour
2 tsp ground ginger

2 egg yolks
1 tsp ground mixed spice
2 tsp bicarbonate of soda

Decoration:

450g/1lb royal icing mix
1 packet coloured candies

1 hour preparation
10 minutes baking per sheet
Makes 1 house

1 Draw and cut out templates (see page 252) on card as follows: two roof pieces 15x20cm/6x8 inches. Two sides 6x20cm/2¹/₂x8 inches. Two gables 11x17cm/4x6¹/₂ inches, rising to a point. One chimney piece 5cm/2 inches deep, two chimney sides 5cm/2 inches deep with a sloping side. One chimney piece 2x5cm/³/₄x2 inches.

2 Preheat the oven to 190°C/375°F/Gas 5. Put the sugar, syrup, treacle and margarine in a pan and heat gently until melted. Sift the flour, ginger, mixed spice and bicarbonate of soda into a bowl. Stir in the egg yolks and the melted mixture.

3 Knead to a soft dough. Halve the dough and keep half covered. While still warm, roll the dough out between two

sheets of non-stick paper. Lift the top paper away and cut around the card template. Lift excess pastry from the paper. Place the gingerbreads on the paper on a baking sheet and bake for 8-10 minutes. Leave flat on the paper to cool. Repeat with remaining trimmings and dough.

4 When all the pieces are cold and stiff, assemble the house. Make up the royal icing mix and pipe along the wall edges. Join the walls together on a cake board, press and leave to set. Fix on the roof pieces and then the chimney. Pipe on decorative icing to resemble snow. Decorate the roof with sweets.

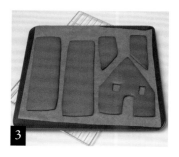

Chocolate Mousse Cake

Quick and Easy

This party gateau looks complicated, but it is easy to make. Just swirl the two sets of whipped cream on top for a marbled effect.

Ingredients:

2 tablespoons cocoa
175g/6oz soft margarine
175g/6oz golden caster
**   sugar**
3 eggs
175g/6oz self-raising flour
1 tsp baking powder
2 tbsp plain yogurt

Filling and Topping:

450ml/¹/₂pt whipping cream
75g/3oz dark chocolate,
**   melted**

30 minutes preparation
25 minutes baking
Serves 8

1 Preheat the oven to 180°C/350°F/Gas 4. Grease and line the bases of two 19cm/7¹/₂ inch sandwich tins with non-stick baking paper.

2 In a large bowl, blend the cocoa with 3 tablespoons of boiling water, then cool. Add the remaining cake ingredients to the bowl and beat for 2 minutes until smooth.

3 Divide between the tins, smooth level and bake for 20-25 minutes until springy. Cool on a wire rack.

4 For the filling and topping, whip the cream until firm, then divide between two bowls. Add the melted chocolate to one bowl and stir until blended. Spread a little chocolate cream on to one sponge layer and use to sandwich the cakes.

5 Spoon alternate tablespoons of chocolate cream and plain cream on top of the cake. Roughly swirl with a palette knife to make a marbled pattern. Refrigerate until served.

Cook's tip:

It is easy to melt the chocolate in a microwave. Break the chocolate into pieces, place in a microwave-proof bowl and use the Low setting.

Black Forest Gateau

Easy Entertaining

1 hour preparation
25 minutes baking
Serves 8

Ingredients:

5 eggs
175g/6oz caster sugar
75g/3oz unsalted butter,
 melted
50g/2oz plain flour
50g/2oz cocoa powder

Filling and Decoration:

225g/8oz plain chocolate,
 melted
425g/15oz can or jar of stoned
 black cherries, drained
4 tbsp kirsch
2 tbsp morello cherry jam
600ml/1pt double cream

1 Preheat the oven to 180°C/350°F/Gas 4. Grease and line the bases of two 20cm/8 inch sandwich tins and dust lightly with flour.

2 Place the eggs and sugar in a large bowl set over a pan of hot water and whisk continuously until thick and pale, for about 5 minutes. Remove from the heat. Continue whisking for about 10 minutes until the mixture cools and falls in a thick ribbon.

3 Cool the melted butter. Sift the flour and cocoa into the mixture, then fold in gently. Pour the butter into the mixture in a slow stream and fold in.

4 Divide the mixture between the tins and bake for about 25 minutes until springy to the touch. Cool in the tins for 15 minutes, then turn out on to a

wire rack. When completely cold, cut each cake in half horizontally.

5 Spread the melted chocolate out on a clean surface in a thin layer. When just setting, pull a long thin-bladed knife across the chocolate at an angle and, in a sawing action, scrape the chocolate into thin curls. Repeat using all the chocolate.

6 Spread the cut sponges with cream and sandwich together. Place one on a serving dish, spread with jam. Scatter over half the cherries, top with cream and place the remaining cake on top. Sprinkle the top cake with kirsch, then cover the whole cake with the remaining cream. Press the chocolate curls on to the sides. Decorate the top with cherries and flakes.

White Chocolate Gateau

Party Special

This delicate gateau is smothered in a delightful white chocolate cream. It is delicious served with fresh strawberries or raspberries in the summer.

Ingredients:

50g/2oz white chocolate
175g/6oz butter or block margarine
175g/6oz caster sugar
3 eggs, beaten
175g/6oz self-raising flour
Finely grated zest of ½ a lemon

Filling and Topping:

150ml/¼pt whipping cream
3 tbsp chocolate nut spread
225g/8oz white chocolate
200ml/7fl oz crème fraiche

30 minutes preparation
20-25 minutes baking
Serves 8

1

1 Preheat the oven to 180°C/350°F/Gas 4. Grease and line the bases of two 19cm/7½ inch sandwich tins with non-stick baking paper. Grate the white chocolate finely.

2 Place the butter and sugar in a bowl and beat with an electric mixer until soft and fluffy. Gradually add the eggs, using a little flour with each addition. Fold in the flour, zest and grated chocolate.

3 Spoon into the tins and spread level. Bake for 20-25 minutes until golden and just firm to the touch. Turn out to cool on a wire rack.

4 For the filling, whip the whipping cream until stiff, then divide in half. Mix half with the chocolate nut spread and use to sandwich the cakes together.

5 For the topping, break the white chocolate into pieces and melt in the microwave on Low. Alternatively, melt in a bowl set over a pan of warm water. Beat together with the crème fraiche and cool for 5 minutes. When cold, fold in the whipped cream and spread over the top and sides of the cake.

4

5

Gingerbread House

Template

side

Cut out: 2 gable ends (one with a door and windows)
2 roof pieces
2 sides
1 set of chimney pieces

chimney pieces

roof

gable end

index

credits & acknowledgements

I would like to thank Progress Bakeware for supplying the Good Housekeeping range of bakeware and to Mermaid Cookware for the utensils in the step-by-step photography. Also, to Billington's Sugars for supplying their unrefined sugars for baking.

Thanks to Harrison Fisher and Co. (www.premiercutlery.co.uk) for supplying the knives and some of the small kitchen utensils also used in the step-by-step pictures.

Thanks also to Colin Bowling and Paul Forrester and the many cake tasters at Britannia Studios.

THE LITTLE LIBRARY OF EARTH MEDICINE

DEER

Kenneth Meadows

Illustrations by Jo Donegan

DORLING KINDERSLEY
LONDON • NEW YORK • SYDNEY • MOSCOW

A DORLING KINDERSLEY BOOK

Managing editor: Jonathan Metcalf
Managing art editor: Peter Cross
Production manager: Michelle Thomas

The Little Library of Earth Medicine was
produced, edited and designed by
GLS Editorial and Design
Garden Studios, 11-15 Betterton Street
London WC2H 9BP

GLS Editorial and Design
Editorial director: Jane Laing
Design director: Ruth Shane
Project designer: Luke Herriott
Editors: Claire Calman, Terry Burrows, Victoria Sorzano

Additional illustrations: Roy Flooks 16, 17, 31; John Lawrence 38
Special photography: Mark Hamilton
Picture credits: American Natural History Museum 8-9, 12, 14-15, 32

First published in Great Britain in 1998
by Dorling Kindersley Limited
9 Henrietta Street, London WC2E 8PS

2 4 6 8 10 9 7 5 3 1

A CIP catalogue record for this book is available from the British Library

UK ISBN 0 7513 0516 2   AUSTRALIAN ISBN 1 86466 033 3

Reproduced by Kestrel Digital Colour Ltd, Chelmsford, Essex
Printed and bound in Hong Kong by Imago

CONTENTS

INTRODUCING
EARTH MEDICINE

To Native Americans, medicine is not an external substance but an inner power that is found in both Nature and ourselves.

E arth Medicine is a unique method of personality profiling that draws on Native American understanding of the Universe, and on the principles embodied in sacred Medicine Wheels.

Native Americans believed that spirit, although invisible, permeated Nature, so that everything in Nature was sacred. Animals were perceived as acting as

messengers of spirit. They also appeared in waking dreams to impart power known as "medicine". The recipients of such dreams honoured the animal species that appeared to them by rendering their images on ceremonial and everyday artefacts.

NATURE WITHIN SELF

Native American shamans – tribal wisemen – recognized similarities between the natural forces prevalent during the seasons and the characteristics of those born

Shaman's rattle
Shamans used rattles to connect with their inner spirit. This is a Tlingit shaman's wooden rattle.

"Spirit has provided you with an opportunity to study in Nature's university." Stoney teaching

during corresponding times of the year. They also noted how personality is affected by the four phases of the Moon – at birth and throughout life – and by the continual alternation of energy flow, from active to passive. This view is encapsulated in Earth Medicine, which helps you to recognize how the dynamics of Nature function within you and how the potential strengths you were born with can be developed.

Animal ornament
To the Anasazi, who carved this ornament from jet, the frog symbolized adaptability.

MEDICINE WHEELS

Native American cultural traditions embrace a variety of circular symbolic images and objects. These sacred hoops have become known as Medicine Wheels, due to their similarity to the spoked wheels of the wagons that carried settlers into the heartlands of once-Native American territory. Each Medicine Wheel showed how different objects or qualities related to one another within the context of a greater whole, and how different forces and energies moved within it.

One Medicine Wheel might be regarded as the master wheel because it indicated balance within Nature and the most effective way of achieving harmony with the Universe and ourselves. It is upon this master Medicine Wheel (see pp.10–11) that Earth Medicine is structured.

Feast dish
Stylized bear carvings adorn this Tlingit feast dish. To the American Indian, the bear symbolizes strength and self-sufficiency.

THE MEDICINE WHEEL

The outer Wheel is divided into twelve birth times, each of which has its own animal totem, and stone, tree, and colour affinities.

At the hub of the Wheel, surrounded by representations of Elements, Directions, and energy flow, is the Wakan-Tanka — symbol of invisible energies coming into physical reality.

Season of birth
Each of the twelve segments relates to a specific time of year (see pp.12–13).

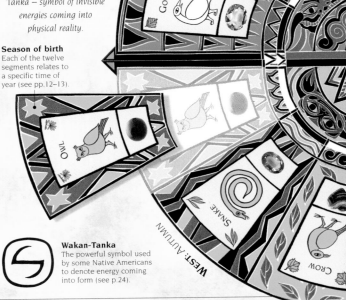

NORTH: WINTER

WOLF

OTTER

GOOSE

OWL

SNAKE

CROW

WEST: AUTUMN

Wakan-Tanka
The powerful symbol used by some Native Americans to denote energy coming into form (see p.24).

Stone affinity
Each birth time has a particular stone associated with it (see pp.14–15).

Tree affinity
Each birth time is connected to a type of tree (see pp.14–15).

Birth totem
An animal totem represents each birth time (see pp.16–17).

Directional totem
One of four cardinal Directions exerts an influence on each birth time (see pp.18–19).

Principal Element
Each birth time is fundamentally influenced by one of the four Elements (see pp.20–21).

Energy flow
Energy alternates between active and receptive with each birth time (see p.24).

Elemental Aspect
Each birth time has its own Elemental Aspect (see pp.20–21).

EAST: SPRING

SOUTH: SUMMER

FALCON

BEAVER

DEER

DEER

WOODPECKER

SALMON

BROWN BEAR

11

THE TWELVE
BIRTH TIMES

THE STRUCTURE OF THE MEDICINE WHEEL IS BASED UPON THE SEASONS TO REFLECT THE POWERFUL INFLUENCE OF NATURE ON HUMAN PERSONALITY.

The Medicine Wheel classifies human nature into twelve personality types, each corresponding to the characteristics of Nature at a particular time of the year. It is designed to act as a kind of map to help you discover your strengths and weaknesses, your inner drives and instinctive behaviours, and your true potential.

The four seasons form the basis of the Wheel's structure, with the Summer and Winter solstices and the Spring and Autumn equinoxes marking each season's passing. In Earth Medicine,

Seasonal rites
Performers at the Iroquois mid-Winter ceremony wore masks made of braided maize husks. They danced to attune themselves to energies that would ensure a good harvest.

each season is a metaphor for a stage of human growth and development. Spring is likened to infancy and the newness of life, and Summer to the exuberance of youth and of rapid development. Autumn represents the fulfilment that mature adulthood brings, while Winter symbolizes the accumulated wisdom that can be drawn upon in later life.

Each seasonal quarter of the Wheel is further divided into three periods, making twelve time segments altogether. The time of your birth determines the direction from which

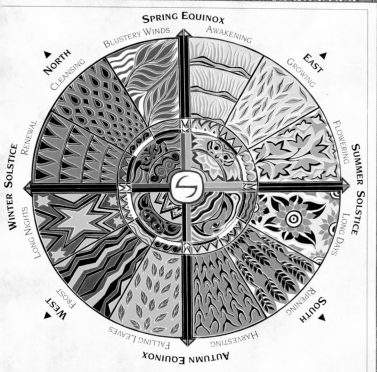

SPRING EQUINOX

BLUSTERY WINDS AWAKENING

NORTH
Cleansing

EAST
Growing

Renewal

Flowering

Winter Solstice

Summer Solstice

Long Nights

Long Days

WEST
Frost

Ripening

SOUTH
Harvesting

Falling Leaves

AUTUMN EQUINOX

THE TWELVE TIME SEGMENTS

you perceive life, and the qualities imbued in Nature in that season are reflected in your core character.

Each of the twelve time segments, or birth times, is named after a feature in the natural yearly cycle. For

example, the period after the Spring equinox is called Awakening time because it is the time of new growth, while the segment after the Autumn equinox is named after the falling leaves that characterize that time.

13

THE SIGNIFICANCE OF TOTEMS

NATIVE AMERICANS BELIEVED THAT TOTEMS — ANIMAL SYMBOLS — REPRESENTED ESSENTIAL TRUTHS AND ACTED AS CONNECTIONS TO NATURAL POWERS.

A totem is an animal or natural object adopted as an emblem to typify certain distinctive qualities. Native Americans regarded animals, whose behaviour is predictable, as particularly useful guides to categorizing human patterns of behaviour.

A totem mirrors aspects of your nature and unlocks the intuitive knowledge that lies beyond the reasoning capacity of the intellect. It may take the form of a carving or moulding, a pictorial image, or a token of fur, feather, bone, tooth, or claw. Its presence serves as an immediate link with the energies it represents. A totem is therefore more effective than a glyph or symbol as an aid to comprehending non-physical powers and formative forces.

PRIMARY TOTEMS

In Earth Medicine you have three primary totems: a birth totem, a Directional totem, and an Elemental totem. Your *birth totem* is the embodiment of core characteristics that correspond with the dominant aspects of Nature during your birth time.

Symbol of strength

The handle of this Tlingit knife is carved with a raven and a bear head, symbols of insight and inner strength.

All twelve birth totems, each relating to a birth time, are described on pp.16–17.

Your *Directional totem* aligns you with your inner senses, which direct the main thrust of your endeavours. Each of the four seasons on the Wheel is compatible with one of the four Directions, and each of the Directions is represented by a totem. For example, Spring is associated with the East, where the sun rises, and signifies seeing things in new ways; its totem is the Eagle. The four

Prize totem
A chief or warrior of the Fox tribe affirmed his rank with this bear claw necklace.

Directional totems are explained on pp.18–19.

Your *Elemental totem* relates to your instinctive behaviours. The qualities of the four Elements – Fire, Water, Earth, and Air – and their totems are introduced on pp.20–21.

THREE AFFINITIES
Each birth time also has an affinity with a tree, a stone, and a colour (see pp.36–41). These three affinities have qualities that can strengthen you during challenging times.

"*If a man is to succeed, he must be governed not by his inclination, but by an understanding of the ways of animals...*" Teton Sioux teaching

THE TWELVE
BIRTH TOTEMS

THE TWELVE BIRTH TIMES ARE REPRESENTED BY TOTEMS,
EACH ONE AN ANIMAL THAT BEST EXPRESSES THE
QUALITIES INHERENT IN THAT BIRTH TIME.

Earth Medicine associates an animal totem with each birth time (the two sets of dates below reflect the difference in season between the northern and southern hemispheres). These animals help to connect you to the powers and abilities that they represent. For an in-depth study of the Deer birth totem, see pp.28–29.

FALCON
21 March–19 April (N. Hem)
22 Sept–22 Oct (S. Hem)
Falcons are full of initiative, but often rush in to make decisions they may later regret. Lively and extroverted, they have enthusiasm for new experiences but can sometimes lack persistence.

DEER
21 May–20 June (N. Hem)
23 Nov–21 Dec (S. Hem)
Deer are willing to sacrifice the old for the new. They loathe routine, thriving on variety and challenges. They have a wild side, often leaping from one situation or relationship into another without reflection.

BEAVER
20 April–20 May (N. Hem)
23 Oct–22 Nov (S. Hem)
Practical and steady, Beavers have a capacity for perseverance. Good homemakers, they are warm and affectionate but need harmony and peace to avoid becoming irritable. They have a keen aesthetic sense.

WOODPECKER
21 June–21 July (N. Hem)
22 Dec–19 Jan (S. Hem)
Emotional and sensitive, Woodpeckers are warm to those closest to them, and willing to sacrifice their needs for those of their loved ones. They have lively imaginations but can be worriers.

SALMON
22 July–21 August (N. Hem)
20 Jan–18 Feb (S. Hem)

Enthusiastic and self-confident, Salmon people enjoy running things. They are uncompromising and forceful, and can occasionally seem a little arrogant or self-important. They are easily hurt by neglect.

BROWN BEAR
22 August–21 Sept (N. Hem)
19 Feb–20 March (S. Hem)

Brown Bears are hardworking, practical, and self-reliant. They do not like change, preferring to stick to what is familiar. They have a flair for fixing things, are good-natured, and make good friends.

CROW
22 Sept–22 Oct (N. Hem)
21 March–19 April (S. Hem)

Crows dislike solitude and feel most comfortable in company. Although usually pleasant and good-natured, they can be strongly influenced by negative atmospheres, becoming gloomy and prickly.

SNAKE
23 Oct–22 Nov (N. Hem)
20 April–20 May (S. Hem)

Snakes are secretive and mysterious, hiding their feelings beneath a cool exterior. Adaptable, determined, and imaginative, they are capable of bouncing back from tough situations encountered in life.

OWL
23 Nov–21 Dec (N. Hem)
21 May–20 June (S. Hem)

Owls need freedom of expression. They are lively, self-reliant, and have an eye for detail. Inquisitive and adaptable, they have a tendency to overextend themselves. Owls are often physically courageous.

GOOSE
22 Dec–19 Jan (N. Hem)
21 June–21 July (S. Hem)

Goose people are far-sighted idealists who are willing to explore the unknown. They approach life with enthusiasm, determined to fulfil their dreams. They are perfectionists, and can appear unduly serious.

OTTER
20 Jan–18 Feb (N. Hem)
22 July–21 August (S. Hem)

Otters are friendly, lively, and perceptive. They feel inhibited by too many rules and regulations, which often makes them appear eccentric. They like cleanliness and order, and have original minds.

WOLF
19 Feb–20 March (N. Hem)
22 August–21 Sept (S. Hem)

Wolves are sensitive, artistic, and intuitive – people to whom others turn for help. They value freedom and their own space, and are easily affected by others. They are philosophical, trusting, and genuine.

THE INFLUENCE OF THE
DIRECTIONS

ALSO KNOWN BY NATIVE AMERICANS AS THE FOUR
WINDS, THE INFLUENCE OF THE FOUR DIRECTIONS IS
EXPERIENCED THROUGH YOUR INNER SENSES.

Regarded as the "keepers" or "caretakers" of the Universe, the four Directions or alignments were also referred to by Native Americans as the four Winds because their presence was felt rather than seen.

DIRECTIONAL TOTEMS

In Earth Medicine, each Direction or Wind is associated with a season and a time of day. Thus the three Spring birth times – Awakening time, Growing time, and Flowering time –

all fall within the East Direction, and morning. The Direction to which your birth time belongs influences the nature of your inner senses.

The East Direction is associated with illumination. Its totem is the Eagle – a bird that soars close to the Sun and can see clearly from height. The South is the Direction of Summer and the afternoon. It signifies growth and fruition, fluidity, and emotions. Its totem, the Mouse, symbolizes productivity, feelings, and an ability to perceive detail.

"Remember...the circle of the sky, the stars, the supernatural Winds breathing night and day...the four Directions." Pawnee teaching

SPRING EQUINOX

NORTH

EAST

WINTER SOLSTICE

SUMMER SOLSTICE

WEST

SOUTH

AUTUMN EQUINOX

BUFFALO

EAGLE

GRIZZLY BEAR

MOUSE

The four Directions

Each Direction is associated with a season and a time of day, and also with a principal function: the East with determining, the South with giving, the West with holding, and the North with receiving.

The West is the Direction of Autumn and the evening. It signifies transformation – from day to night, from Summer to Winter – and the qualities of introspection and conservation. Its totem is the Grizzly Bear, which represents strength

drawn from within. The North is the Direction of Winter and the night, and is associated with the mind and its sustenance – knowledge. Its totem is the Buffalo, an animal that was honoured by Native Americans as the great material "provider".

THE INFLUENCE OF THE ELEMENTS

THE FOUR ELEMENTS — AIR, FIRE, WATER, AND EARTH —
PERVADE EVERYTHING AND INDICATE THE NATURE OF
MOVEMENT AND THE ESSENCE OF WHO YOU ARE.

lements are intangible qualities that describe the essential state or character of all things. In Earth Medicine, the four Elements are allied with four fundamental modes of activity and are associated with different aspects of the self. Air expresses free movement in all directions; it is related to the mind and to thinking. Fire indicates expansive motion; it is linked with the spirit and with intuition. Water signifies fluidity; it

Elemental profile
*The Elemental config-
uration of Deer is Air of
Fire. Fire is the Principal
Element and Air the
Elemental Aspect.*

WATER

AIR

EARTH

AIR

FIRE

EARTH

has associations with the soul and the emotions. Earth symbolizes stability; it is related to the physical body and the sensations.

ELEMENTAL DISTRIBUTION

On the Medicine Wheel one Element is associated with each of the four Directions – Fire in the East, Earth in the West, Air in the North, and Water in the South. These are known as the Principal Elements.

The four Elements also have an individual association with each of the twelve birth times – known as the Elemental Aspects. They follow a cyclical sequence around the Wheel based on the action of the Sun (Fire) on the Earth, producing atmosphere (Air) and condensation (Water).

The three birth times that share an Elemental Aspect belong to the same Elemental family or "clan", with a totem that gives insight into its key characteristics. Deer people belong to the Butterfly clan (see pp.34–35).

ELEMENTAL EMPHASIS

For each birth time, the qualities of the Elemental Aspect usually predominate over those of the Principal Element, although both are present to give a specific configuration, such as Fire of Earth (for Deer's, see pp.34–35). For Falcon, Woodpecker, and Otter, the Principal Element and the Elemental Aspect are identical (for example, Air of Air), so people of these totems tend to express that Element intensely.

FIRE

EARTH

AIR

FIRE

WATER

WATER

THE INFLUENCE OF THE MOON

THE WAXING AND WANING OF THE MOON DURING ITS
FOUR PHASES HAS A CRUCIAL INFLUENCE ON THE
FORMATION OF PERSONALITY AND HUMAN ENDEAVOUR.

Native Americans regarded the Sun and Moon as indicators respectively of the active and receptive energies inherent in Nature (see p.24), as well as the measurers of time. They associated solar influences with conscious activity and the exercise of reason and the will, and lunar influences with subconscious activity and the emotional and intuitive aspects of human nature.

The Waxing Moon

This phase lasts for approximately eleven days. It is a time of growth and therefore ideal for developing new ideas and concentrating your efforts into new projects.

The Full Moon

Lasting about three days, this is when lunar power is at its height. It is therefore a good time for completing what was developed during the Waxing Moon.

THE FOUR PHASES

There are four phases in the twenty-nine-day lunar cycle, each one an expression of energy reflecting a particular mode of activity. They can be likened to the phases of growth of a flowering plant through the seasons: the emergence of buds (Waxing Moon), the bursting of flowers (Full Moon), the falling away of flowers (Waning Moon), and the germination of seeds (Dark Moon). The influence of each phase can be felt in two ways: in the formation of personality and in day-to-day life.

The energy expressed by the phase of the Moon at the time of your birth has a strong influence on personality. For instance, someone born during the Dark Moon is likely to be inward-looking, whilst a person born during the Full Moon may be more expressive. Someone born during a Waxing Moon is likely to have an outgoing nature, whilst a person born during a Waning Moon may be reserved. Consult a set of Moon tables to discover the phase the Moon was in on *your* birthday.

In your day-to-day life, the benefits of coming into harmony with the Moon's energies are considerable. Experience the energy of the four phases by consciously working with them. A Native American approach is described below.

The Waning Moon
*A time for making changes, this phase lasts
for an average of eleven days. Use it to
improve and modify, and to dispose of what
is no longer needed or wanted.*

The Dark Moon
*The Moon disappears from the sky for
around four days. This is a time for
contemplation of what has been achieved,
and for germinating the seeds for the new.*

THE INFLUENCE OF
ENERGY FLOW

THE MEDICINE WHEEL REFLECTS THE PERFECT BALANCE OF THE COMPLEMENTARY ACTIVE AND RECEPTIVE ENERGIES THAT CO-EXIST IN NATURE.

Energy flows through Nature in two complementary ways, which can be expressed in terms of active and receptive, or male and female. The active energy principle is linked with the Elements of Fire and Air, and the receptive principle with Water and Earth.

Each of the twelve birth times has an active or receptive energy related to its Elemental Aspect. Travelling around the Wheel, the two energies alternate with each birth time, resulting in an equal balance of active and receptive energies, as in Nature.

Active energy is associated with the Sun and conscious activity. Those whose birth times take this principle prefer to pursue experience. They are conceptual,

outgoing, practical, energetic, and analytical. Receptive energy is associated with the Moon and subconscious activity. Those whose birth times take this principle prefer to attract experience. They are intuitive, reflective, emotional, conserving, and nurturing.

THE WAKAN-TANKA

At the heart of the Wheel lies an S-shape within a circle, the symbol of the life-giving source of everything that comes into physical existence – seemingly out of nothing. Named by the Plains Indians as Wakan-Tanka (Great Power), it can also be perceived as energy coming into form and form reverting to energy in the unending continuity of life.

DEER MEDICINE

YOUR IN-DEPTH PERSONALITY PROFILE

SEASON OF BIRTH
FLOWERING TIME

THE ENERGIZING POWER OF SPRING REACHES ITS PEAK
DURING THE THIRD BIRTH TIME OF THE SEASON, LENDING
THOSE BORN THEN THE POWER OF RAPID CHANGE.

Flowering time is one of the twelve birth times, the fundamental division of the year into twelve seasonal periods (see pp.12–13). As the last segment of the Spring cycle, it is a time in which the creative and generative power of Nature is at its height. The trees are in full leaf and many flowers are blooming in the bright, still-lengthening days of this splendid, sensuous time of year.

INFLUENCE OF NATURE

The qualities and characteristics imbued in Nature at this time form the basis of your own nature. So, just as Nature is transforming the Earth, if you were born during Flowering time you too have an inner urge and ability to change whatever comes within your reach. This power might be directed at situations, yourself, or other people.

Your temperament will match the warmth and unpredictability of the season. Just as the influence of the Sun on the Earth is moving towards its peak, you will possess an intensity that enables you to express your creativity rapidly and energetically. However, like a sultry day at this time of year, you are prone to moodiness if beset by setbacks and disappointments that frustrate your efforts to grow. Then, your normally affectionate nature can assume a coolness and standoffishness that can be extremely hurtful to those people who are closest to you.

STAGE OF LIFE

This time of year might be compared to the inquisitive and adventurous nature of youth on the eve of adulthood, when action is taken with determination and courage but often without the understanding that comes with experience and age.

In human development terms, it is a period of life when knowledge is keenly sought after; a time of increasing awareness of the scope and complexity of the world and humanity. Consequently, your warm, affectionate, and eager nature seeks variety and enormous sensory input.

ACHIEVE YOUR POTENTIAL

You are always searching for opportunities to stretch your senses and expand your awareness, so you can comprehend more fully how you fit into the greater scheme of things

Nature's energy

The creative and transforming power of Nature reaches its zenith in this, the last cycle of Spring before the Summer solstice. Many varieties of flowers are blooming and deciduous trees are in full leaf.

and how you can achieve your full potential. Try to use your intuition to open up your understanding beyond the immediate and obvious.

Although you demonstrate abundant vitality when your interest is aroused or when a project is new, you can become lethargic when pressed to complete mundane and routine matters. Set your agile mind and enthusiastic nature to finding ways to motivate yourself to complete tasks you find boring.

"Life is a circle from childhood to childhood; so it is with everything where power moves." Black Elk teaching

BIRTH TOTEM
THE DEER

THE ESSENTIAL NATURE AND CHARACTERISTIC BEHAVIOUR OF THE DEER EXPRESSES THE PERSONALITY TYPE OF THOSE BORN DURING FLOWERING TIME.

Like the deer, people born during Flowering time are congenial, adaptable, sensitive, and expressive. If you were born at this time, you love variety and thrive on challenges, often giving far more than is expected of you. You appreciate beautiful objects and have expensive tastes. Although both mentally and physically dextrous,

you get bored easily and are readily diverted from routine tasks. A good communicator, you are charming and sociable, and enjoy working as part of a team. You make lively and engaging company, although you can unnerve others by your tendency to change direction suddenly.

You lack patience, persistence, and commitment, which leads you to leap from one relationship or job to another before you have gained all you can from them and without reflecting sufficiently on the consequences of your move. Also, your highly sensitive nature makes you prone to moodiness and irritability.

You are constantly active and like to live on your nerves but this can lead to physical and

mental exhaustion. Even when you
are not physically occupied, your
mind is busy, making it difficult for
you to relax fully. It is essential that
you find ways to unwind and ensure
that you get enough sleep.

HEALTH MATTERS

Try not to ignore symptoms
of poor health, especially if
they relate to your most
vulnerable areas, which are the lungs
and bronchial passages. If you do
develop a cough, take care to prevent
it from developing into bronchitis.

Deer power

Sensitive, lively, and charming, the deer also
expresses the nervous and changeable
aspects of the versatile and quick-witted
people born at this time.

THE DEER AND
RELATIONSHIPS

SOCIABLE AND ENGAGING, DEER PEOPLE ARE USUALLY
POPULAR. THEY MAKE LIVELY AND CONSIDERATE
PARTNERS BUT MAY PROVE FICKLE IN LOVE.

Naturally friendly creatures, Deer people, like their totem animal, enjoy the company of members of their own sex. If your birth totem is Deer, you make a considerate and compassionate friend, who is seldom demanding and usually sensitive to the difficulties of others. However, you like to talk, tending to know a little about a lot, and to have an answer for almost everything. In consequence, most of your friends tend to be good listeners.

LOVING RELATIONSHIPS

Although Deer people need love and affection, they do not like to be smothered. Blatantly flirtatious, male Deer exudes charm, while female Deer can be tempestuous and alluring. Both male and female Deer

enjoy sex like some people enjoy a good meal, and you are happy to take the sexual initiative.

When problems in relationships arise, it is generally because of your restless and moody nature or your mercenary attitude. For, while you are willing to share most things, money is not one of them. You also tend to be self-indulgent.

COPING WITH DEER

Deer people are impatient, emotional, and vulnerable, so don't be too intense when putting across your point of view to them. They dislike dogmatism and being told what to do and what to think. So the best way to handle Deer – as a friend, lover, employer, or employee – is to cultivate a friendly, informal, and relaxed attitude.

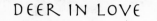

DEER IN LOVE

Deer with Falcon Deer's lively and inventive nature complements Falcon's passion and determination, so both should thrive.

Deer with Beaver Deer's easy-going and restless nature may disturb Beaver's desire for security.

Deer with Deer A lively and adventurous pairing, which will run smoothly if both can learn to work together at the same speed.

Deer with Woodpecker This makes a lively pairing. Woodpecker can overcome Deer's self-centredness; Deer can inject a sense of fun and purpose.

Deer with Salmon Both are practical opportunists, so they can be unscrupulous together. Their similarities may result in mutual irritability at times.

Deer with Brown Bear Deer's high-spirited vigour can work well with Brown Bear's eye for detail and determination.

Deer with Crow Both are loyal and realistic enough to accept each other's shortcomings.

Deer with Snake Although Snake can be good-natured and considerate, Deer may have difficulty coping with Snake's intensity.

Deer with Owl Deer may find Owl's protectiveness difficult to handle, while Owl may find Deer a little selfish and inconsiderate.

Deer with Goose Deer's freedom-loving nature may resent Goose's zest for disciplined dedication.

Deer with Otter These two vibrant and affable personalities can bond well by doing everything together.

Deer with Wolf Wolf can be an inspiration to Deer if they are dedicated to each other and devoted to achieving similar goals.

DIRECTIONAL TOTEM
THE EAGLE

THE EAGLE SYMBOLIZES THE INFLUENCE OF THE EAST
ON DEER PEOPLE, WHO LOOK TOWARDS THE FUTURE AND
LIVE LIFE ACCORDING TO THEIR PRINCIPLES.

Eagle mask
*This Tlingit shaman's
headdress represents the
eagle, which is associated
with being far-sighted.*

A wakening time, Growing time, and Flowering time all fall within the quarter of the Medicine Wheel that is associated with the East Direction or Wind.

The East is aligned with Spring and the dawn of the new day, and it is therefore associated with new beginnings, openness, illumination, and revival. The power of the East's influence is primarily with the spirit, and its principal function is the power of determining. It takes as its totem the soaring, far-sighted eagle.

The specific influence of the East on Deer people is on perception, enabling correct choices to be made. The East Wind in this period may be likened to the early experiences of life, and to the qualities of fearlessness and action. It is also associated with the ability to transcend any problems.

EAGLE CHARACTERISTICS

The eagle can fly high in the sky, so Native Americans associated it with lofty ideals and high principles – and with illumination gained from coming closer to the spirit and the source of life. It is also a bird that can

The spirit of the East

The Sun rises in the East, symbolizing
new beginnings; the Eagle totem
signifies enlightenment
and decisiveness.

perceive small objects from long distances, so it is associated with the ability to look ahead and take decisive action. The eagle can also soar far, wide, and high above the land, allowing it to appreciate the landscape as a whole as well as picking out particular details.

If your Directional totem is Eagle you are likely to be strongly principled. You will also have an independent and adventurous spirit, which is always keen to seek out fresh approaches. Your thinking will be towards the future, and you will have the ability to stand back from the detail and make sense of the overall pattern. In addition, your ability to see into the heart of things will enable you to choose wisely and act firmly and decisively.

ELEMENTAL TOTEM
THE BUTTERFLY

LIKE THE BUTTERFLY, WHICH FLITS FROM PLACE TO PLACE, DEER PEOPLE'S RESTLESS TEMPERAMENT REQUIRES VARIETY AND ROOM TO MANOEUVRE.

The Elemental Aspect of Deer people is Air. They share this Aspect with Crow and Otter people, who all therefore belong to the same Elemental family or "clan" (see pp. 20–21 for an introduction to the influence of the Elements).

THE BUTTERFLY CLAN

Each Elemental clan has a totem to provide insight into its essential characteristics. The totem of the Elemental clan of Air is Butterfly, which symbolizes a quick, lively, restless, and changeable nature.

The butterfly flits here and there, seeking variety, and settling only where the atmosphere is harmonious.

Free to change

The butterfly symbolizes the fundamental quality of the Element of Air: free movement.

34

So, if you belong to this clan, you will have a lively personality and be constantly on the move – physically, mentally, and emotionally.

Quick-witted, thoughtful, and imaginative, you are full of ideas, which you are keen to communicate to others. You dislike being restricted either physically or mentally. You are quick and impatient, and crave stimulation and plenty of opportunity to express yourself.

ELEMENTAL PROFILE

For Deer people, the predominant Elemental Aspect of changeable Air is fundamentally affected by the qualities of your Principal Element – enthusiastic Fire. Consequently, if you were born at this time, you are likely to have an abundance of energy together with a bright, sparkling personality, which is bent on effecting changes in your circumstances and surroundings.

Air of Fire
The Element of Air feeds Fire, generating enthusiasm and expansiveness.

You may have a tendency to bound ahead of yourself, driven by the enthusiasm of Fire and the urge to change that is inherent in Air. So it is that you sometimes find yourself in situations for which you are ill-prepared. When faced with setbacks arising from these situations, you can become moody and lethargic.

At times like these, or when you are feeling low or lacking in energy, try the following revitalizing exercise. Find a quiet spot outside, away from the polluting effects of traffic and the activities of others, and, for several minutes, breathe slowly and deeply.

With each in-breath, acknowledge that you are drawing into yourself the energizing power of the life-force, which is being absorbed by every cell of your being, revitalizing and refreshing your whole body.

STONE AFFINITY
AGATE

BY USING THE GEMSTONE WITH WHICH YOUR OWN ESSENCE RESONATES, YOU CAN TAP INTO THE POWER OF THE EARTH ITSELF AND AWAKEN THE ABILITY YOU NEED.

Gemstones are minerals that are formed within the Earth itself in an exceedingly slow but continuous process. Native Americans valued gemstones not only for their beauty but also for being literally part of the Earth, and therefore possessing part of its life-force. They regarded gemstones as being "alive" – channellers of energy that could be used in many ways: to heal, to protect, or for meditation.

Every gemstone has a different energy or vibration. On the Medicine Wheel, a stone is associated with each birth time, the energy of which

Polished agate

This highly polished oval agate clearly displays the layered and wavy banding peculiar to this gemstone, which occurs in a wide variety of colours.

resonates with the essence of those born during that time. Because of this energy affiliation, your gemstone can be used to help bring you into harmony with the Earth and to create balance within yourself. It can enhance and develop your good qualities and endow you with the qualities or abilities you need.

ENERGY RESONANCE

Deer people have an affinity with agate – a form of chalcedony with a distinctive banded appearance, which varies tremendously in colour and pattern. Agate has a dual nature: it can deflect disturbing vibrations

ACTIVATE YOUR GEMSTONE

Obtain a slice of agate and cleanse it by holding it under cold running water. Allow it to dry naturally, then, holding the stone with both hands, bring it up to your mouth and blow into it sharply and hard three or four times in order to impregnate it with your breath. Next, hold it firmly in one hand and silently welcome it into your life as a friend and helper.

When you are faced with a problem to solve or a choice to make, use the agate to help you meditate on the issue. Find a quiet spot to sit without fear of interruption and take the piece of sliced agate in your right hand – your "activity" hand. Focus your thoughts on the problem and, with the help of your affinity stone, seek a solution. Listen for the still, small voice of your inner self.

and resentments caused by humans or the environment, and it can attract positive energies. Regarded as a healing stone by Native Americans, agate is particularly linked to material need and practical matters. This gemstone is also thought to attract loyalty.

If your birth totem is Deer, agate is especially useful in stabilizing your ever-fluctuating emotions. It also enhances your intuitive abilities, making it a valuable aid when trying

to ascertain the best time to begin a new enterprise at work or at home, or the most effective time to make a fundamental change to your life situation.

Agate power

To benefit most from its effect, wear agate next to your skin in the form of a ring, pendant, or necklace.

"The outline of the stone is round; the power of the stone is endless." *Lakota Sioux teaching*

TREE AFFINITY
ALDER

GAIN A DEEPER UNDERSTANDING OF YOUR OWN NATURE
AND AWAKEN POWERS LYING DORMANT WITHIN YOU BY
RESPECTING AND CONNECTING WITH YOUR AFFINITY TREE.

Trees have an important part to play in the protection of Nature's mechanisms and in the maintenance of the Earth's atmospheric balance, which is essential for the survival of the human race.

Native Americans referred to trees as "Standing People" because they stand firm, obtaining strength from their connection with the Earth. They therefore teach us the importance of being grounded, whilst at the same time listening to, and reaching for, our higher aspirations. When respected as living beings, trees can provide insight into the workings of Nature and our own inner selves.

On the Medicine Wheel, each birth time is associated with a particular kind of tree, the basic qualities of which complement the nature of those born during that time. Deer people have an affinity with the alder. Essentially a waterside tree, it is therefore associated with the "watery" qualities of emotional energies, which can be fast-flowing and at times turbulent.

CONNECT WITH YOUR TREE

Appreciate the beauty of your affinity tree and study its nature carefully, for it has an affinity with your own nature.

The common alder is a hardy, fast-growing tree, with smooth, lustrous, dark-green leaves that last well into the Autumn. At home beside rivers, it thrives in both poor soils and wet conditions, even growing in standing water.

Try the following exercise when you need to revitalize your inner strength. Stand beside your affinity tree. Place the palms of your hands on its trunk and rest your forehead on the backs of your hands. Inhale slowly and let energy from the tree's roots flow through your body. If easily available, obtain a cutting or twig from your affinity tree to keep as a totem or helper.

A key inherent strength of the alder is its water-resistance, which is due to the oiliness of the wood. Consequently, in times of emotional stress, Deer people can tap into their own powers of resistance by connecting with their tree (see panel above).

EMOTIONAL YET RESILIENT

If your birth totem is Deer, you have a sensitive nature and a tendency towards moodiness during times of stress. This can often provoke you into unconsidered and emotional responses to situations or people. Your feelings at such a time can be so strong as seemingly to carry you along in their current.

However, just as the water-resistant wood of the alder can withstand the pressure of troubled waters, so you can find the power to manage emotional pressures with fortitude. Call on the alder's help and draw on its energy; its resilient quality will renew your inner strength.

"All healing plants are given by Wakan-Tanka; therefore they are holy." Lakota Sioux teaching

COLOUR AFFINITY
ORANGE

Enhance your positive qualities by using the power of your affinity colour to improve your emotional and mental states.

Each birth time has an affinity with a particular colour. This is the colour that resonates best with the energies of the people born during that time. Exposure to your affinity colour will encourage a positive emotional and mental outlook, while colours that clash with your affinity colour will have a negative effect on your sense of well-being.

Orange resonates with Deer people. Made up of equal parts yellow and red, it combines the influence of both these colours. Yellow is associated with the mind, and red with vitality and passion, so orange is the embodiment of youthful liveliness,

Colour scheme

Let an orange colour theme be the thread that runs through your home, from the table settings to the walls and floors.

BREATHE IN YOUR COLOUR

Take a piece of pale orange or peach-coloured paper, card, or fabric. Place it near an open window where it can be seen, and stand directly before it with your legs slightly apart, so that your weight is evenly distributed.

Focus on the colour and inhale slowly through the nose. Imagine that the air you breathe in is the colour of the card. Hold the breath for a few seconds and feel that colour filtering through your entire body, energizing every cell. Breathe out slowly and deliberately. Pause, then begin the sequence again. Continue this rhythmic colour breathing for three or four minutes to feel the positive effects.

suggestive of energy, enthusiasm, and ambition. It is a cheerful and optimistic colour that invigorates and stimulates creativity. It arouses courage and daring in the drive for exploration and accomplishment.

COLOUR BENEFITS

Strengthen your aura and enhance your positive qualities by including shades of orange – peach, apricot, russet – in the interior decor of your home. Spots of colour can make all the difference. A peach-tinted lampshade, for example, can alter the ambience of a room, or try filling a bronze vase with deep orange Chinese lanterns.

If you need a confidence boost, wear something that contains orange. Whenever your energies are low, practise the colour breathing exercise outlined above to balance your emotions, awaken your creativity, and help you to feel joyful.

> "The power of the spirit should be honoured with its colour." Lakota Sioux teaching

WORKING THE WHEEL
LIFE PATH

CONSIDER YOUR BIRTH PROFILE AS A STARTING POINT IN
THE DEVELOPMENT OF YOUR CHARACTER AND THE
ACHIEVEMENT OF PERSONAL FULFILMENT.

ach of the twelve birth times is associated with a particular path of learning, or with a collection of lessons to be learned through life. By following your path of learning, you will develop strengths in place of weaknesses, achieve a greater sense of harmony with the world, and discover inner peace.

YOUR PATH OF LEARNING
For Deer people, the first lesson on your path of learning is to overcome

impulsiveness. Because of your impatience and your desire to be always on the move, you have a tendency to prefer to do anything rather than nothing. This can sometimes result in your making snap decisions that can be disconcerting to friends and colleagues alike. Next time you have to decide on a course of action try not to be so hasty.
Consider all the

"Each man's road is
shown to him within his
own heart. There he sees all
the truths of life." *Cheyenne teaching*

options carefully. Compare the situation with a similar one in the past, and, if possible, consult all the relevant people. Then evaluate the information and make your decision.

Deer people also need to learn how to discern what is of true value from that which has only limited or short-term benefits. Try not to be deceived by appearances: what seems promising at first glance is often disappointing in the long term.

Your third lesson is to cultivate a more disciplined and consistent approach to life, and to enjoy the accomplishment

of tasks. Your lack of patience with routine and with those less quick-witted than yourself can mean that you do not get the best out of your work or your colleagues, and that you are tempted to change jobs too often to achieve your full career potential. Equally, your fickleness may hamper your ability to find fulfilment in a loving relationship.

WORKING THE WHEEL
MEDICINE POWER

HARNESS THE POWERS OF OTHER BIRTH TIMES TO TRANSFORM YOUR WEAKNESSES INTO STRENGTHS AND MEET THE CHALLENGES IN YOUR LIFE.

The whole spectrum of human qualities and abilities is represented on the Medicine Wheel. The totems and affinities associated with each birth time represent the basic qualities with which those born at that time are equipped.

Study your path of learning (see pp.42–43) to identify those aspects of your personality that may need to be strengthened, then look at other birth times to discover the totems and affinities that will assist you in this task. For example, your Elemental profile is Air of Fire (see pp.34–35), so for balance you need the stabilizing qualities of Earth and

Complementary affinity

A key strength of Owl – weak in Deer – is the ability to see clearly in times of uncertainty.

the adaptive nature of Water. Brown Bear's Elemental profile is Earth of Water and Snake's is Water of Earth, so meditate on those birth totems. In addition, you may find it useful to study the profiles of the other two members of your Elemental clan of Butterfly – Crow and Otter – to discover how the same Elemental Aspect can be expressed differently.

Also helpful is the birth totem that sits opposite yours on the Medicine Wheel, which contains qualities that complement or enhance your own. This is known as your complementary affinity, which for Deer people is Owl.

ESSENTIAL STRENGTHS

Described below are the essential strengths of each birth totem. To develop a quality that is weak in yourself or that you need to meet a particular challenge, meditate upon the birth totem that contains the attribute you need. Obtain a representation of the relevant totem – a claw, tooth, or feather; a picture, ring, or model. Affirm that the power it represents is within you.

Falcon medicine is the power of keen observation and the ability to act decisively and energetically whenever action is required.

Beaver medicine is the ability to think creatively and laterally – to develop alternative ways of doing or thinking about things.

Deer medicine is characterized by sensitivity to the intentions of others and to that which might be detrimental to your well-being.

Woodpecker medicine is the ability to establish a steady rhythm throughout life and to be tenacious in protecting all that you hold dear.

Salmon medicine is the strength to be determined and courageous in the choice of goals you want to achieve and to have enough stamina to see a task through to the end.

Brown Bear medicine is the ability to be resourceful, hardworking, and dependable in times of need and to draw on inner strength.

Crow medicine is the ability to transform negative or non-productive situations into positive ones and to transcend limitations.

Snake medicine is the talent to adapt easily to changes in circumstances and to manage transitional phases well.

Owl medicine is the power to see clearly during times of uncertainty and to conduct life consistently, according to long-term plans.

Goose medicine is the courage to do whatever might be necessary to protect your ideals and adhere to your principles in life.

Otter medicine is the ability to connect with your inner child, to be innovative and idealistic, and to thoroughly enjoy the ordinary tasks and routines of everyday life.

Wolf medicine is the courage to act according to your intuition and instincts rather than your intellect, and to be compassionate.